A MANUAL FOR INTERMEDIATE & ADVANCED SEA KAYAKERS

SEA KAYAK

GORDON BROWN

 Pesda Press LTD

www.pesdapress.com

Front cover: *Paddling out through the surf, North Skye.*

Back cover: *Resting in a basalt cave south of Loch Bracadale, Skye.*

First published in Great Britain 2006 by Pesda Press

Tan y Coed Canol

Ceunant

Caernarfon

Gwynedd

LL55 4RN

Reprinted 2007
Reprinted 2009
Reprinted 2010
Reprinted 2013
Reprinted 2017

© Copyright 2006 Gordon Brown

ISBN-10: 0-9547061-7-X
ISBN-13: 9780954706173

Printed and bound in Poland, www.hussarbooks.pl

ABOUT THE AUTHOR

Gordon Brown is quick to admit that he has the best job in the world, kayaking almost every day from his home on the Isle of Skye.

His first career was as a car mechanic, working in his father's garage in Ayrshire, although his first love was always kayaking. In this, his first book, Gordon draws upon thirty years of sea kayaking and coaching experience, from early days exploring Scotland's west coast in a home-built wood and canvas kayak, to paddling in Greenland, New Zealand, Tasmania, Sri Lanka, Norway, Iceland, Canada and the USA. He spent three months coaching on the rivers of Nepal and has kayaked throughout the United Kingdom, including all the outlying islands. This wealth of knowledge, supplemented by forays into whitewater and surf coaching, has been distilled into the pages of this book.

Gordon owns and runs Skyak Adventures with his wife Morag. As well as introducing novices to the sport in one of the most beautiful yet challenging parts of the world, Gordon trains and assesses to the highest level within the British Canoe Union. He is helping to develop a new awards scheme for the BCU and remains Scotland's only American Canoe Association advanced open water instructor.

It is surely difficult to disagree with Gordon's own assessment. He probably does have the best job in the world!

Photo: Morag Brown.

Acknowledgements

This book would not have been possible without the generous support of many people, too many to list, but you know who you are. Thank you.

However, I must single out some for special mention: The team at Pesda Press for encouragement, advice and hard work; Lendal for excellent paddles; Valley Sea Kayaks for their continued support; Knoydart Kayaking Systems and Kokatat for clothing; and Reed Chillcheater for coping with my strange requests!

Finally, and most of all I'm hugely grateful to all of my family, and especially my wife Morag, for support, advice, inspiration and for allowing me the time to write... and to kayak.

All photos by Gordon Brown, except where noted. Photographic contributors; Morag Brown, Duncan Winning, Simon Willis, Douglas Wilcox, Trys Burke, Les Wilson, Jeff Allen, Johan Wagner, Franco Ferrero, Alun Hughes, Nigel Dennis, the Shetland Museum and the Norwegian National Library.

CONTENTS

PLATE 1 *Sea kayaking means many things to many people.*
Photo of Penrhyn Mawr by Alun Hughes.

1 What is Sea Kayaking?

A sport, a specialist activity - it is much more than that… originating in the Arctic as a means of travel and as a way of hunting for food, things have moved on a bit from then. For a complete view we must transport ourselves back in time. It is twilight at midday in the early Arctic autumn, never completely dark due to the reflections off the snow and ice; you haven't seen the sun for some days now and it will not show its head above the southern horizon for many months. Your family is unsure if the catch from the summer will see you all through the winter. Your kayak is in the crook of your arm as you carry it towards the icy water, the carved 'masik' falling at the balance point and another carved deck beam at the right place for your hand to grasp. These familiar feelings have been learnt from years of this ritual.

Your kayak was custom-built for you by the kayak builder in the village, his skills handed down from his father and grandfather. Three times your arm span for the length, your hips when seated plus two fingers on each side for the beam, the deck profile to suit the prevailing conditions and the purpose for which the kayak was to be used. Generally a low, flat deck contour was selected for hunting and also for travelling especially when there were big seas to contend with.

This low deck made for a good working area where important tools were kept, harpoon on the right (if you were right-handed), throwing stick for the harpoon under the deck cords, line support for the harpoon line on the front deck forwards of your paddling area. A sealskin bladder float was carried on the rear deck.

fig. 1.1 An Inuit paddling a kayak in heavy seas. Pen and ink drawing by Andreas Bloch, 1889. From the book Paa ski over Grønland by Fridtjof Nansen.

Jump forward in time by millennia (or a mere hundred years)…

Think how easy it is for us. We go into a retail therapy unit, pick which colour we like and furnish the therapist with lots of our hard-earned cash. This is assuming that we know which kayak we like, that it suits our planned use and fits us reasonably well. We go home and wait for the phone call to tell us it is ready for collection, job done!

fig. 1.2 Ken Taylor paddles the kayak he returned with from his expedition to Greenland in 1959. Built by Emanuele Kornielsen of Igdlorssuit on the west coast of Greenland. Measurements taken from this kayak influenced the design of a great many of the modern British kayaks. Photo: Duncan Winning

7

We don't have to think too much about maintenance, certainly not the re-skinning every year or two. We can even bump into things without too much worry that there will be a gaping hole in the structure.

Nowadays we use our craft for very different purposes, sometimes we fish and hunt from them but most of the time they are used for our recreation. We do not have to go out in all weathers in order that our families will survive.

The quality time we spend in our kayaks is really great, no telephone (unless you leave your mobile switched on), no computer, and no real distractions. It can be just you, the boat and your surroundings – the best therapy that you cannot afford. Of course you can choose to go out with a group of friends or even folk you haven't met. What is important is that you have the skills necessary to handle yourself and your kayak to the best of your abilities. The only way you can gain these skills is to get out and make good use of your time on the water. There are very few people who are able to learn something from first principles without having given it a go.

Because the sea is an alien environment, we have to make sure we take precautions. As with almost every other outdoor pursuit, there is good sense in going out with at least two other paddlers of similar ability, and for most of us this would be ideal. Sometimes you make the decision to go kayaking alone; this choice should never be undertaken lightly and you should prepare for this day.

**Become aware of the moods of the sea,
the interaction of the water against rock,
the effects of the weather and tides.**

**Know how your kayak behaves in a variety of conditions
and also how you respond,
and you will take steps towards becoming
an accomplished sea kayaker…**

THE SELKIE

As with all oral traditions, folklore is passed generation to generation until someone is able to write
down some 'definitive' version. The late John Heath,
scholar of Inuit kayaks and people, told me of the
high probability of truth in this piece of Scottish
coastal folklore.

The Selkie is a being from the sea, half man – half
seal. When he came ashore he was able to go back
to the sea if he still had his sealskin but if the sealskin was stolen then he would be unable to return.
Stories about this mythological creature would have
been much embellished but the factual basis remains
– imagine that the sealskin was not just any old sealskin but a kayak and tuilik (anorak); the mythical
creature could conceivably be a kayaker.

How did he come to be on the west coast of
Scotland? John's theory explains: The Dutch whalers,
having been hunting in the Arctic, took home many
curios, the greatest of these being a kayak along with
kayaker. It was illegal to smuggle people into Hol-
land so, on sight of land, the man was put back into
his kayak and he came ashore close to the whaler's
route. This explains the many tales in Scotland or the
north-east of England of a kayaker paddling into a
harbour, being taken out of his kayak and looked after. Unfortunately most men died within a few weeks,
probably from tuberculosis or another virulent dis-
ease to which they had not been exposed before.

*fig. 1.3 Half man – half seal, Ken
models in a tuilik, the hem of which
fits tightly around the cockpit, keeping
water from the boat even when
capsized. Photo: Duncan Winning.*

*fig. 1.4 Arctic whaler in Lerwick
harbour. Whaling took off in
Scotland in the 1750s but by
1840 had declined with a collapse
in whale populations and the
introduction of coal gas street
lighting, replacing whale oil.
© Shetland Museum.*

PLATE II *North West Greenland kayak showing wood and canvas construction.*

2 Boat Dynamics

A sea kayak has to be able to travel distances at a reasonable speed and at the same time must be manoeuvrable enough for a spot of rockhopping when working close inshore (or making a landing). In general a short kayak will turn more easily than a long one and a longer kayak will be faster. It must be light but strong – a heavy kayak feels sluggish, while the same design made lighter is an absolute joy to paddle. It is worth a look at some of the variations within sea kayak design to try to gain a bit of understanding about the advantages of each.

2.1 WOOD & CANVAS KAYAKS

These have a limited place within modern sea kayaking. Being the preserve of the Inuit enthusiast these craft are custom-built, usually by the paddler, to more often than not historic plans. Quite often narrow, low volume and with only enough room for the paddler's legs, the majority of these kayaks are made in the Greenland style (a chined hull, low front deck and even lower rear deck). Many of these boats are made purely for Greenland style rolling, which has an increasing following the world over.

fig. 2.1 *Inside a skin kayak. Uncomplicated by bulkheads, thigh braces or even a seat.*

There are even some designs that allow rolling manoeuvres to be performed that could not even be attempted in a 'normal' sea kayak. Being custom-made to fit the paddler has obvious advantages but at a cost to versatility. Around one week of your time will be required to produce a kayak of this type, assuming you have some expert help. With canvas skins rot is a major problem if the kayak cannot be kept inside and dry when not in use.

2.2 PLYWOOD & CEDAR STRIP KAYAKS

These tend to be purely the domain of the amateur woodworker who probably spends more time making his craft than paddling it. Plywood panels are cut to shape and then stitched together with copper wire and nylon line. The shape forms as the stitching is tightened and then the seams are finished with glass fibre.

Cedar strip uses thin lamina of wood, which have been machined with a bead and cove. These are glued and stapled together over a set of formers, prepared to match the shape of the boat to be built. The whole thing, when

fig. 2.2 *A fine example of the complex forms which can be constructed in strip wood.*

finished, is sheathed with glass cloth and epoxy resin. The result of both these methods of construction is a boat which you have built to a design you like with all of your woodworking skills on show. Very few serious sea kayakers use kayaks built this way, although some manufacturers do still prototype with wood.

2.3 POLYETHYLENE KAYAKS

Polyethylene kayaks, made from similar materials as soft drinks bottles, have become the most popular construction. Most are rotomoulded, a process involving a large oven, a measured amount of plastic pellets and a mould which pitches and rolls at the right time, at the right temperature and for the right length of time. The mould when opened releases a kayak with no seams, but more spectacularly, no holes for cockpit or hatches. These have to be cut out. This is an expensive method of building a single kayak but a cheap method for producing very

fig. 2.3 A polyethylene kayak, typically around half the price of a custom made composite kayak.

many. Polyethylene makes a robust kayak with enough rigidity to be of use on moderate trips. Unfortunately most kayaks built this way tend to be heavier and lacking the stiffness and responsiveness of their composite counterparts (triple-layer plastic construction helps to allay this shortcoming). Their major advantage is that, although not quite indestructible, they are able to take knocks that would have composite boat owners trembling.

2.4 COMPOSITE KAYAKS

Composite kayaks are the pride of the fleet, with sweeping lines, gloss finishes and ever more high-tech materials. These kayaks are the choice of most serious sea kayakers. As these are layed up by hand, many manufacturers offer custom bulkhead placement, extra deck fittings and choice of colours. Some companies are using carbon fibre and Kevlar along with high-tech resin transfer techniques to produce lighter but stronger boats. These specialist materials give a high strength-to-weight ratio and are more resistant to impact damage. These space age materials are also very expensive and have a tendency to be less resistant to UV light and abrasion than epoxy glass fibre.

fig. 2.4 An example of a composite kayak.

2.5 ANATOMY OF A SEA KAYAK

Below is a simplified view of a typical sea kayak. Like people, kayaks are not created equal so the differences are sometimes subtle, sometimes not. For want of a better way to describe the anatomy I have used common names which will be referred to throughout the book. I may offend the purist with this use of terminology but I do so for the sake of clarity, (for example there are very few sea kayaks with true chines as the chine was a result of the construction method used). The following topics are not intended to be a completely technical description of how a kayak will behave, but rather a jumping off point for further discussion and experimentation. Naval architects of many years standing still use a wave tank and scale models for testing prototypes, as the relationships between the water and watercraft are extremely complex. I suggest you do the same and take every opportunity to test out these assertions in your own scale model!

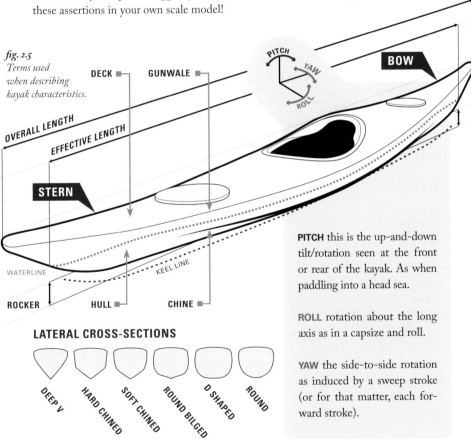

fig. 2.5
Terms used when describing kayak characteristics.

PITCH · YAW · ROLL · BOW · DECK · GUNWALE · OVERALL LENGTH · EFFECTIVE LENGTH · STERN · WATERLINE · KEEL LINE · ROCKER · HULL · CHINE

LATERAL CROSS-SECTIONS

DEEP V · HARD CHINED · SOFT CHINED · ROUND BILGED · D SHAPED · ROUND

PITCH this is the up-and-down tilt/rotation seen at the front or rear of the kayak. As when paddling into a head sea.

ROLL rotation about the long axis as in a capsize and roll.

YAW the side-to-side rotation as induced by a sweep stroke (or for that matter, each forward stroke).

The chapter on Canoe, Kayak and Paddle Design in the BCU *Canoe & Kayak Handbook* (2002) is an excellent source of further reading on these topics.

2.6 LENGTH, WIDTH & SPEED

Waterline length - There are different lengths to be taken into consideration. When looking at any kayak you will notice that there either is, or is not, overhang at the ends. If two kayaks of the same overall length are placed side by side in the water and marks are made where the water reaches at each end, generally the one that has the longer waterline length will be the fastest.

fig. 2.6 Overhang on the bow combined with flare helps the boat ride over waves.

◎ Overall length – this is the fixed length of your kayak and is generally what everyone specifies. This is not a good indicator of the effective maximum hull speed.

◎ Length on the waterline – this is a better indicator of speed. A longer waterline generally means a faster kayak and conversely a shorter one suggests a slower (but more manoeuvrable) boat.

Waterline length directly relates to wave resistance, that is to say the wavelength of the bow wave created when paddling forwards is a product of the length of your boat and your speed. As speed increases, it is as if the boat is trying to climb over its own bow wave, a feat not possible under paddle power - so your sea kayak remains in the trough of its own wake (so a sea kayak is a displacement hulled craft, unlike for example a flat-planing hull craft like a surf kayak which uses wave power).

Displacement & width – a wide kayak will displace more water further to each side as it passes forward for a narrower kayak of the same length. Also a finer bow, one that is more pointy, will displace this water more gradually over the length of the kayak, creating less disturbance and reducing resistance.

Skin drag – there is a frictional resistance to forward progress, between the skin of the kayak and the water. This is affected by the wetted area of the kayak – here length, width and lateral cross-section all have a part to play in the ultimate speed of the kayak. A long narrow kayak with a deep V or round hull (which have an efficient surface area to volume ratio) will have less skin drag and therefore be faster than a kayak of the same volume which is shorter, wider and chined or D shaped.

A combination of factors – almost all the characteristics of the hull have a varied effect on displacement, wave resistance and frictional resistance. For example, rocker, the bowing of the keel line of the kayak from the lowest point of the hull to its tips, also affects speed. Extreme rocker will create more overhang, shortening the waterline, and also increase wetted area. But a little rocker is valuable to give greater directional agility.

Indeed all of these characteristics have costs and benefits in areas other than maximum hull speed too. The difference between overall length and waterline length is related to the freeboard – the amount of boat that is still above the water when you are sitting in the cockpit and all of your equipment is secured in or on the kayak. Little freeboard means a wetter time when you are on the water if there is any size of sea running. A lot of freeboard will hamper your paddling and the kayak will be adversely affected by any wind.

2.7 WATERLINE TEMPLATE

As the hull's waterline length differs from its overall length, so too the hull's waterline template (outline shape) differs from the overall hull shape. Again, it is the waterline shape which is significant as to how fast the kayak is and how easily it turns in the water.

A sea kayak hull is rarely symmetrical fore to aft, they generally have their widest point behind the cockpit. This is often referred to as Swedish form, in contrast to hulls which have their widest point somewhere forward of the centre, which are Fish form. It can be said with some assurance that this distinction is somewhat unhelpful as it too brings together competing factors which affect speed and handling, so I shall pass swiftly on.

That said, a sea kayak hull is usually symmetrical about its centre line, until you edge or lean your kayak. This is where the idea of waterline template becomes a dynamic factor. Other dynamic factors include waves, rough water, wind and currents (which are dealt with in more detail in later chapters), but let's consider simply moving about in our boat first.

fig. 2.7 The demonstrable effect of edging – both kayaks being paddled parallel, on the application of edging the upper kayaker veers to the left, still using only forward paddle strokes.

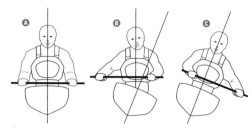

2.8 EDGE, LEAN & TRIM

This is where your body starts to affect the behaviour of your boat

fig. 2.8
Ⓐ *Upright*
Ⓑ *Edge*
Ⓒ *Lean*

- ◎ **Edge** – body stays upright but lower body works to make kayak sit at an angle relative to the surface of the water. Edging is when we put weight onto one buttock and let the opposite knee fine-tune the angle of roll of the kayak. cf. **Body separation** - upper and lower body parts moving independently of each other.

- ◎ **Lean** – body leans towards water with hips locked in line with upper body. Greater body lean equals greater roll of the kayak hull.

- ◎ **Trim** – generally referred to as the fore-to-aft and side-to-side weight distribution of a loaded sea kayak. Too heavy at either end will turn a docile kayak into a beast.

Some folks talk about moving body weight forwards to change trim – it doesn't do much in a sea kayak. If you are very flexible you will be able to move about 10% of your body weight forward by about 30cm when you are seated. One litre (1kg) of water at the end of the kayak has a similar effect on your trim to 8 litres (8kg) at a bulkhead. Therefore, even if you weigh 80 kilos, moving 10% of your weight (8kg) a mere 30cm forward of the balance point will have a negligible effect.

Trim will affect how deep your kayak lies in the water, more weight in the bow and the stern will start to rise. Aside from the effects on displacement and waterline, lifting of the stern can increase the windage on this area; combine this with the lifting from the water of your keel line and you can imagine that the kayak will become very difficult to paddle in a wind and it will lose its track.

2.9 TRACK, CARVE & SKID

- ◎ **Tracking** – can be thought of as the tendency of the hull shape to continue travelling in a straight line and resist turning. A deep V'd hull and straight deep keel line will increase the tendency to track in a straight line; curved or rockered chines and flat areas will increase the tendency to turn.

◎ **Carving** – when the kayak is tilted and the shape of its curved edges (chines or gunwales) in the water cause it to turn a radius determined by that shape (and the asymmetric waterline template created). This enables a lean towards the inside of a turn - much the same as when you turn a corner on a bicycle. A hard chined hull mostly performs in this manner. cf. **Engage edge** – to lean or edge a kayak, bringing the edge into effect.

◎ **Drift / Skid** – drift and skid can be used interchangeably. The opposite to tracking. Practically, in a straight-running sea kayak this can be observed at the rear of the kayak as a turn progresses. Generally most sea kayaks will skid at the rear when tilted to the outside of the turn. This motion can be heard as a gurgling noise coming from the rear. cf. **Edge release** – to lean or edge a kayak, decreasing the effect of an edge.

2.10 STABILITY

There is most definitely a point at which, when you lean your kayak, you will no longer remain upright. Many people, myself included, talk knowledgeably about the different aspects of balance and stability displayed by a kayak, we actually know very little about it. Stability too is an amalgamation of many different components, static or dynamic.

If we sit on a chair with all legs on the floor it is a stable platform, if we put that same chair on two legs and swing on it, it becomes less stable. We can keep the chair in balance by moving our body weight over the balance point. If we now transfer this to a kayak floating on water, we find the following happens:

Firstly when our body weight is positioned over the centre of buoyancy (CB) the kayak feels stable. If we move our weight to the side then our centre of gravity (CG) moves outside the CB and the kayak feels slightly less stable.

If we now put our weight well over, the CB is constrained by the edge of the kayak, this means that the kayak will fall over unless we do something to stop it.

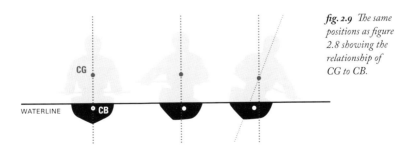

fig. 2.9 The same positions as figure 2.8 showing the relationship of CG to CB.

When the kayak is completely inverted with you in the cockpit it is at its most stable, your CG is suspended below the CB. The next most stable position is the kayak upright with you in the cockpit, your CG is directly above the CB. Least stable is when the kayak is completely on its side and you are in the cockpit with your hips fixed, this position has your CG as far as it is possible to go to the side of the CB.

From this:

◎ Initial stability is the first feelings of the kayak beneath you and whether it feels 'stable' or not.

◎ Secondary stability refers to how stable the kayak feels when it is put on edge.

◎ Dynamic stability is similar to the feeling that you get when you are on a bike. Centrifugal force has an influence as does pressure and drag.

Lateral cross section has an obvious effect on stability. To summarise:

Chined hulls – the traditional shape of the majority of Inuit craft. A keel, two chine stringers and two gunwales make the shape what it is. With a high initial stability feel to it, when leaned there comes a point when there is less kayak to go into the water, so stability decreases. Less effort is required to put this design on an edge but good balance is required to keep it there. For enthusiasts of Greenland rolling this type of kayak is the chosen craft, not only because the form is correct, but also the design allows manoeuvres to be performed that are all but impossible in any other shape of kayak. Low secondary stability makes it much easier to right a capsize. The website qajaqusa.org is a good internet resource for this type of paddling.

Round hulls – feel the most initially unstable. This feeling changes when there is sufficient freeboard, which when the kayak is leaned comes into effect and the buoyancy in this area provides uplift that resists the overturning effect (increasing secondary stability).

Flat bottomed – feel initially stable (on flat water), in general terms they are wider than the others. This means that the outsides of the kayak are buoyant until the kayak is edged. When put onto an edge there comes a point where all of that buoyancy has been submerged, and the boat now becomes unstable. To hold a boat of this type on edge takes a large amount of skill, strength and body control.

D shape – sits somewhere between round and slab sided in terms of stability.

Although most women lack the outright strength of men, they do have other assets that place them well to be able to perform in a sea kayak. As a greater proportion of their weight carried lower on the body means a lower centre of gravity, the advantages are obvious. Generally, being more flexible allows for better blade placement, this together with the low C of G reduces the chance of a capsize. High performance kayaks will be a better fit and feel more stable. This, in turn, means that the average woman's strength disadvantage may well become an advantage, due to the increased efficiency of the hull.

2.11 FITTING OUT YOUR KAYAK

Many people buy kayaks that are far too big for them, this may be in the false belief that 'it's for expeditioning'. For most of the time your kayak will be almost empty, with day or weekend kit and the occasional one or two week journey throughout the year.

An empty kayak will sit much higher on the water than a fully laden one. Similarly, a bigger kayak will sit higher on the water and will be affected more by the wind than a smaller one. If you have to think about ballasting your kayak for most of your time on the water then it is too big for you. This will place a constraint on your paddling.

fig. 2.10 Lower volume kayak with heavier paddler (top left) vs higher volume kayak with lighter paddler (top right). The amount of freeboard and hence windage is noticeably different. Below these are the same kayaks, this time with the same paddler in the seat. A good way to get an initial impression of the size of a kayak is to sit in it and feel for the top of your pelvis, is this above or below the top of the cockpit rim?

Check the position of the top of your pelvis relative to the cockpit rim. If it is below then the boat is most likely too big for you, edging will be difficult, forward paddling will be less efficient and you will probably knock your funny bone on the cockpit rim more times than you'll care to count. You will also end up paddling with your shoulders shrugged, using most of the muscles of your upper body just to sit in the kayak before you even start to paddle. If your pelvis is above the cockpit rim then the boat will handle as its designer intended. You will be able to edge as far as your flexibility will allow.

Obviously some form of padding can be added to the top side of the seat, this will bring your pelvis to a better height but will also reduce the stability of your boat a bit. Another effect of raising the height of the seat is to effectively lower the knee or thigh braces. This can make the cockpit uncomfortable by forcing your knees into a lower position and therefore straighter and closer together. This, in itself, is not a problem but most of us find this seating position awkward and limiting in performance paddling.

HEIGHT OF REAR OF COCKPIT:

The height of the cockpit rim behind you can be critical if you use a back deck roll. Some cockpits have very high rims and while this can be used as an additional backrest, it can also cause a lot of problems as you are forced into rolling in a dynamic, forward position. With a low rear rim it is possible to lie back to roll, but if it is too low then water can gather and seep through your spraydeck onto your clothing and you constantly end up with a cold, damp kidney area.

WIDTH/BEAM:

With larger kayaks, there is a high chance that you will have to use a longer paddle to reach the water. This in itself is not a problem, but longer means heavier and heavier means more work. If the kayak is very wide then any forward stroke you use automatically becomes a turning stroke, due to the blade being further away from the centre line of the boat. You'll end up doing a series of sweep strokes that make the kayak wiggle its way across the water. There is no kayak which will travel in an absolutely straight line, but by limiting the amount of yaw we introduce, we become much more efficient.

A wider kayak will most likely have a wider seat. This means that either: we have to have a wider backside, or, more practically, apply some padding to the sides of the seat. This padding should ensure you are a snug fit but not too tight. You want to be able to 'feel' the kayak through your hips but not be completely restrained by it.

There is a school of thought which recommends having a very loose fit. This allows you to move around more within the cockpit area but obviously gives you less contact with the boat. Imagine being able, with the kayak weathercocking on a long crossing, to move your body weight to one side in order to induce an edge. This would result in you not having to paddle continuously on one side and would reduce fatigue from holding your knee under the deck. However, it would make any of the more high-performance skills more difficult due to you having little grip on the kayak.

HEIGHT OF FOREDECK:

A few years ago, when I was still at school, I was at an outdoor centre on the Isle of Arran when they received their fleet of sea kayaks. Being from two different companies meant that there were different fittings, one lot of boats had holes drilled through the deck for lines and elastics but the others had really nice stainless steel fittings which took great chunks out of my hands. With the nice new boats getting covered with blood, it wasn't long before these fittings were removed and holes drilled in the same way as the other kayaks had. I still have the scars more than thirty years later!

Now almost all manufacturers use some type of recessed deck fitting which reduces the chance of similar mutilation happening to an unsuspecting paddler.

A larger kayak means a higher foredeck, which also means a higher paddling action. While this high action is not bad, it can be difficult to adjust to especially as your shoulders will have to do quite a bit more work than they would with a lower deck. There is also more chance of knocking your hands on the deck or other pieces of equipment located there. If the kayak is particularly large in relation to your size, then the amount of it that is above the water will be affected so much by the wind as to make it almost impossible to paddle in anything other than a light breeze.

COCKPIT SIZE:

Some paddlers using the smaller ocean-style cockpit firmly believe that they have more security and better control of their kayak. However with the thought that manufacturers have put into the fitting out of the larger keyhole style cockpit these arguments fall down. The choice is ultimately yours, both have benefits and both have drawbacks.

The ocean cockpit is more difficult to get in and out of in a hurry. If you have big feet and long legs you will probably have to use your paddle for support. However if like me, your sight is getting worse as the years go on, the benefit of having your chart closer to you cannot be understated. It is also possible to have a lot more equipment on your front deck but this is not necessarily a good idea.

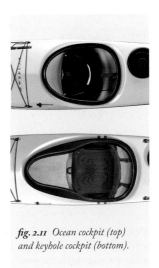

fig. 2.11 Ocean cockpit (top) and keyhole cockpit (bottom).

With a keyhole cockpit your chart will be a bit further away unless you have a spraydeck that has tie-on points for a chart case. A chart on your spraydeck can be an encumbrance but it does mean that even when you are out of your boat you will still have your chart attached to you. The ease of getting in and out from a keyhole cockpit in a hurry cannot be understated. It is, for most people, easy to sit down onto the seat, paddle away from where you have launched and then slide your legs in one at a time and then fix your spraydeck in place. Pumping out is also a lot easier as is drying the cockpit area with a sponge. The old argument of the spraydeck imploding when a wave crashes onto you is completely dismissed by the strength and stretch qualities of the materials used in making spraydecks these days.

2.12 SKEGS

fig. 2.12 Retractable skeg.

Generally most kayaks, when evenly loaded, will weathercock, that is turn into the wind. Imagine having a device that you could use to counteract this turning, and free your efforts into going in a straight line rather than paddling only on one side.

A correct marine definition of a skeg is that of an immovable fin at the rear of the vessel and that of a rudder is a vertically hinged blade, mounted at the rear of the vessel, that is used to steer. However, the practical modern retractable skeg is adjustable.

Several years ago some manufacturers fitted a skeg to their designs, the result was that these kayaks would only go downwind. This was not a lot of use unless that is where you wanted to travel. This skeg meant that the packing, or trim, of the kayak had to be just right or it became a bit of a pig.

A variable fin was then designed and this could be deployed from the cockpit by a variety of means. Quickly becoming known as a retractable skeg, most systems use a flexible stainless steel braided cable to pull the skeg up into the recess, which is fine. These same systems also use the same cable to push the skeg into the deployed position. This is similar to placing a piece of rope on the ground and trying to push it. The rope will kink and so will a skeg control wire if forced against any resistance.

Retractable skegs are now fitted to the majority of sea kayaks in the UK; in the main they are not designed into the kayak but fitted almost as an afterthought.

The purpose of the retractable skeg is to trim your kayak to the conditions. Some systems have become so advanced that you would need a degree in metallurgy, with the bolt on extras of aeronautical engineering as well as hydraulics, just to work out what was happening. Ideally whichever method of deployment is used should be field maintainable by a paddler of limited mechanical aptitude (when on expedition it's sensible to take a spare cable together with the tools necessary to carry out a replacement). Simple is generally best.

Like most boys when they start to drive, the skeg control is used as an on-off switch in much the same way as the accelerator pedal. It takes a bit of time to get used to applying the skeg by degree. That said, the general position of a retractable skeg will be: Down to go downwind – up to go upwind – somewhere between up and down when the wind is coming from the side. Perhaps a better way to remember the position is to push the control to where the wind is coming from relative to your heading.

2.13 RUDDERS

Rudders when fitted to sea kayaks are an oft abused piece of equipment; most paddlers use them as the main turning device instead of using their skill as a paddler. A rudder provides an additional means to turn the kayak, as well as additional tracking similar to a skeg. However a rudder will usually impede a very tight turn with the kayak right on edge and in a rough sea the rudder can spend as much time out of the water as it does in it! Furthermore the many parts of a rudder from footrest to hinge are prone to damage and require maintenance. Some kayaks are designed with the use of a rudder in mind (often race kayaks where it allows the paddler to concentrate completely on making the kayak go forwards rather than steering with the paddle) but most kayaks will perform better with the application of sophisticated use of the paddle rather than use of a rudder. As with a retractable skeg, simple is best, and remember to carry spare parts with you. An extra control cable could save a lot of grief on anything more than a couple of hours paddle.

fig. 2.13 Overstern rudder *with internal control cables, which can be lifted clear of the water by a third line.*

PLATE III *Leaving Loch Coruisk, Skye. In my opinion, the best one-day paddle in the world.*

3 Paddle Design

Paddles come in very many forms and equally many materials. For the serious sea kayaker however there is much less choice.

Most sea kayakers will own a paddle that they enjoy using so much that they are much more likely to change their kayak before their paddle. These same people will probably give you a go of their kayak but might well be a bit reticent of handing over their beloved paddle. A good paddle, which is suited to the type of paddling you do, is not too heavy or light, has a comfortable diameter of shaft as well as blades of suitable size and shape, will feel like nothing in your hands and should always feel that way. Weight is a major consideration and has a direct effect on cost – the more you pay the lighter the paddle becomes. Some other important variables are:

- ◎ **Blade material**: wood, nylon, glass fibre, carbon.

- ◎ **Blade shape**: symmetric, asymmetric, semi-wing, wing.

- ◎ **Blade area**: infinitely variable within sensible limits.

- ◎ **Feather**: the angle of offset between the blades.

- ◎ **Shaft material**: wood, fibreglass, carbon, carbon/kevlar mix.

- ◎ **Shaft diameter**: small for small hands, large diameter for larger hands.

- ◎ **Shaft shape**: straight or crank (if crank shaft, distance between thumbs is important due to your grip being 'fixed' by the location of the crank), indexing of grip, width of shoulders.

With this amount of choice there is a good chance that you will not hit on the right combination first time. However, it is possible to get close to what you want, and having a few adjustments means that you can begin to appreciate the subtle differences 2cm extra length or 20° less feather angle makes over the course of a day.

Fig. 3.1 Feathers of 90°, 30° and 0°. This affects the degree of wrist flexion required, the windage of the non-active blade and the behaviour of the paddles whilst rolling. Your chosen shaft may also influence your choice of feather.

3.1 MODIFIED CRANK

The majority of sea kayakers now use this type of shaft. Working like a castor on a chair, the blade trails the hand that is pulling to lock it into the water. This means that you do not have to grip the shaft much at all and reduce the likelihood of overuse injuries (see Chapter 4 Preparing Mind & Body). By moving your hand away from the centre line of the shaft you increase your leverage. A much bigger benefit is the extra control and feedback you receive from the paddle as it moves through the water when you perform more vertical strokes. But with ergonomically designed shafts, there are so many variables involved that it is unfortunately impossible to suggest general selection criteria.

3.2 IT IS TRUE – SIZE DOES MATTER

Blade shape becomes important but perhaps not quite as much as area. Long narrow blades require a low action while short stubby ones demand a higher, more upright stroke. If a low stroke is what you use make sure you use a maximum amount of body rotation.

3.3 LENGTH IS IMPORTANT TOO

Overall paddle length depends on the type of use and normal cadence (stroke rate). If your paddle is too long you will have to use a low action, forcing you to perform a sweep instead of a power stroke. This is not the most efficient method of making your kayak go forwards but it is surprising just how many people put up with it. For a long time the 'you have to use a low action on the sea' camp has been favoured. This is complete rubbish, you should use whatever style of forward technique suits you best for the journey you are doing. That said however, I would recommend that you adopt an effective, efficient and stylish technique and make that your standard. On the few occasions when you are caught out by a strong enough wind to cause 'paddle flutter', you can lower your paddles and adapt your technique to a lower paddling action, just enough to suit the conditions. That way you will be paddling efficiently 95% of the time.

If your paddle is too short, your stroke rate will be much higher. This in itself is not a problem as it means that you will be carrying out more reps at a lesser force, this is not as tiring as it might sound. However, you may have to reach for the water every stroke. This will set up a rolling motion to the kayak which kills your boat speed. Think for a moment about cyclists… they work very hard at maintaining a cadence of between 80 and 90rpm whether they are going up or downhill or even along the flat. To achieve this they have a great many gears to choose from. We don't have this luxury and the only way that we can approximate gears is to put less of our blade into the water, which is completely inefficient.

fig. 3.3 (opposite) A selection of blade sizes, shapes and constructions, including a semi-wing (far left).

Another tool at our disposal comes in the form of an extendable paddle shaft. If you were to start with a shorter than average paddle, say 208cm and have adjustment available to convert it to 218cm, then you have a good range to play with. If you were to start with around 220cm adjustable to be even longer you'll be fighting a losing battle with the paddle.

ADJUSTABLE BREAKDOWN PADDLE:

fig. 3.2 Lendal breakdown paddles, Varilok centre joint (left) with Paddlok removable blades (right)

How do you go about choosing a paddle for yourself? Unfortunately there is no easy answer other than try a few, then buy one that seems to suit you at the moment. Obviously, if you were to buy an adjustable paddle, it would be conceivable to vary the length by up to 15cm and feather from left to right hand and from zero to ninety degrees. A breakdown paddle may also enable you to change blades instead of the entire paddle (should you damage a blade, you would only have one to replace).

3.4 BLADE SHAPE

For a conventional blade to perform at its best it must stall in the water, we then lever ourselves past this anchor. A larger blade area will stall more readily than a smaller one and a smaller one will slip more readily. Furthermore, a larger blade on a shorter shaft has a similar effect on cadence to having a smaller blade on a longer shaft. As you will be spending a lot of time paddling forwards it is important that your paddle is able to give you what you want. If it is right for you then you will probably not even notice that it is in your hands.

Asymmetric blades have an end profile which allows the blade to be more stable and balanced as it enters the water, on the exit there is also less lifting of water.

Winged blades, as the name suggests, perform in a similar manner to an aircraft wing. As the blade is pulled through the water and the blade tracks away from the boat, lift is generated, increasing forward drive. This type of paddle is unforgiving and is best used for propelling your kayak forwards. To use a wing properly takes around three to four months of training due to the subtle action and the need to train different muscle groups.

Semi-wing blades behave in part much as a wing but it is also possible to perform all of the other strokes you need when journeying and manoeuvring. Again to get the best out of this blade shape your shoulders need to be well developed as the shape is inherently powerful.

Smaller blades on a shorter shaft take away a lot of power although you will be less fatigued due to lighter weight and higher reps. If you have a shaft that is too long and blades that are too large you may aggravate damage to muscles and tendons.

Inuit or Greenland style blades are a specialist part of sea kayaking. They are excellent for rolling using a variety of different methods, as they are generally unfeathered and sized in a way that allows them to be held anywhere. They were also very good as floating stabilisers when messing about with a harpoon and line. However they lack power and flutter easily without a sturdy forward stroke, which many people find disconcerting. They are not the choice of the majority on the oceans whether in tidal races or in big swells, they are however, very good for having a bit of fun.

fig.3.4 Greenland paddle .

For serious sea kayaking it does matter what type of paddle you use. All of this 'if it was good enough for the Inuit it is good enough for me' is going nowhere. The peoples of the far north, who were the best kayakers without doubt, would today use some form of carbon wiggle stick. They were a race of survivors who utilised whatever came their way to make life easier. For instance when screw nails became available they stopped exclusively tying their kayak frames together, when guns became available they preferred these for the initial kill to harpoons and when outboard motors became reliable they stopped using kayaks for hunting in most areas.

Sometimes it is important to keep an eye on ourselves and ask why we are going down a particular road with our skills. If that reason is to obtain a better understanding of the movement patterns involved in executing a particular skill then that can only be good for the advancement of the sport. If we are doing something because that is the way it has been done for many thousands of years, things will stand still forever.

PLATE IV *Almost an Inuit. Duncan Winning using his Greenland paddle amongst icebergs.*

PLATE V *Ice sculptures in Ummannaq Fiord, North West Greenland.*
Icebergs deserve a healthy respect (inset) and a wide berth, as they may
break apart and invert at any moment.

PLATE VI *Performing a warm-up conditions cardiovascular, musculoskeletal and mental systems.*

4 Preparing Mind & Body

4.1 WARM-UP

It would be fair to say that most sea kayakers are typically well out of their teens! They are also usually very self-conscious about doing physical exercises as part of a warm-up on the beach before going out. There is another way – gentle forward paddling for a period of time during which you gradually increase the intensity until you begin to perspire, can only be good for you. If you then start to look at ensuring you have the full range of mobility required for your planned day by including some gentle stretches this will help prevent injuries. If you plan to launch straight into the surf or a tide race then completing a good warm-up before going afloat will do you no harm. If, when you are afloat, you come across an area where a better warm-up would have been beneficial, stop... then either land or carry out an intense boat-based warm-up which includes some extremes of movement still within the movement zones you know you use.

> I live in a very small village on an island where everyone knows everyone else. When I am running training courses for instructors we, more often than not, look into warm-up and cool-down as well as post-exercise stretching. While this works well inside with no spectators, on the beach is a much nicer place to perform. You can only begin to imagine some of the comments I get from my neighbours when I meet them next!

Doing a warm-up has three main functions. The first is that it prepares your cardiovascular system by increasing your heart rate. This ensures that blood is flowing at a slightly increased temperature and speed throughout your body. Secondly, your musculoskeletal system is prepared for the extra stresses that are about to be placed upon it. By putting your body through all of the movements you are likely to go through when in your kayak there will be less chance of injury to your muscles. The third, and least obvious, purpose of the warm-up is the mental one. By carrying out the physical components you will automatically be getting into the right mindset and preparing your brain for fast reactions if and when you need them.

4.2 BRAIN POWER

The power of your brain is incredible and can prepare your body for exercise just with a couple of cues. I have a friend with experience of almost thirty years of competitive rowing at the top of the Scottish scene, who I'll call Martin because that's his name. He could be sitting at home listening to some music with a resting heart rate of 45bpm and on hearing the word "go", this would jump to over 100bpm within a couple of seconds.

4.3 TRAINING

Although some form of isolated strength, stamina and flexibility training will be valuable, the best exercise for sea kayaking is more sea kayaking. However, it is important to exercise your lower body by running, cycling or somesuch. If you are the sort of person who would rather go to a gym than be outside, then anything that improves your cardiovascular fitness is good. Strength-wise try to go for a holistic approach rather than strengthen only those areas you think will work for pulling and pushing the paddle through the water. Cross training is beneficial as you will be working on different muscle groups than when you kayak; anything which replicates part of the paddling movement will enhance your specific fitness. Rowing is a fantastic whole body exercise and if you look at which muscles are being used you will find that there are very many similarities to those you use when in your kayak.

4.4 OVERUSE INJURIES – TENOSYNOVITIS

Due to the repetitive nature of sea kayaking there is a chance that, sooner or later, you may develop tenosynovitis of the wrist – an inflammation of the fluid-filled sheath (synovium) that surrounds a tendon. This painful complaint, characterised by a grating feeling and persistent pains, can be completely avoided by loosening your grip on the paddle shaft. Prevention is always better than the cure especially if you are on expedition somewhere remote. Treatment for this condition amounts to two weeks or more complete rest of the affected area.

For a long time feathered paddles were thought to have been the cause of 'paddler's-wrist'. More recent studies have shown that it is the side-to-side movement of the wrist that causes inflammation during the paddling motion. By using modified crank paddle shafts (see Chapter 3 Paddle Design) you can do much to reduce this problem. Shaft diameter does have a part to play though, and an inappropriately sized shaft will accelerate its onset. Wearing gloves adds to the effective diameter of your paddle shaft, so for this reason, palmless mitts are a better option.

> **This painful complaint, characterised by a grating feeling and persistent pains, can be completely avoided by loosening your grip on the paddle shaft.**

A light grip on your paddle has other benefits. If you grip tightly, you will be stressing all of your upper body from your fingers to your lower back. Using a loose grip whenever possible allows for an earlier, extended catch, better circulation within your forearms and hands as well as less chance of hot spots or even blisters forming.

4.5 STRETCHING

Stretching after a day on the water is definitely the best way to stop your muscles becoming sore in a couple of days' time. If you sit in a kayak for long you will find that your hamstrings (the muscles and tendons at the back of your thighs) will be tight. If you don't attend to the stretching of these you will become stiff and this will limit your range of movement to apply the forces required for dynamic paddling. So a routine of post paddling stretches will also improve your technique. As with all stretches hold a steady pressure, don't bounce and remember to breathe. Repeat each three times.

SOME LAND-BASED STRETCHES I HAVE FOUND ADVANTAGEOUS:

Mackenzie – This was first shown to me by my physiotherapist when I was working as a motor mechanic, it quickly became a stretch I used every day. When we sit our backs can become rounded which results in poor posture, this compounds itself as lower backache. Lie face down and keeping your pelvis on the floor, push up gently with your hands about shoulder width apart. Hold this position for fifteen seconds ensuring your pelvis stays on the ground. This stretches your quadriceps, lower back and if you look straight ahead then your upper back and neck are subject to a gentle stretch as well.

Cat – This stretch I learned from an osteopath. Like most other kayakers I have problems with the thoracic area of my back and it is notoriously difficult to perform any satisfactory stretch. Leading on from the Mackenzie stretch, move until you are kneeling with your hands on the ground around 50cm in front of your knees. Arch your back as high as you can comfortably go and hold for ten seconds, remembering to breathe.

Wrist & forearm – From the cat stretch, turn your hands so that your thumbs face outwards. Keep your palms in contact with the floor and then gently move your weight backwards until you can feel the stretch work on the inside of your forearm, also stretching your wrist. Hold for twenty seconds.

Yoga bent knee – I first saw this stretch at a coaching conference when a yoga teacher was talking about returning the body to a child-like state, as my mind has never really strayed too far from being a child it works for me. This stretches upper and lower back, rib cage and side of hips, in addition it

is good for your internal organs. A hidden benefit is that having more rotation allows you to look to the rear of the kayak more easily. Sit with your left leg straight. Bend your right leg, cross your right foot over and rest it to the outside of your left knee. Then bend your left elbow and rest it on the outside of your upper right thigh, just above the knee. With your right hand resting behind you, slowly turn your head to look over your right shoulder and at the same time rotate your body to the right. Breathe easily throughout and hold for fifteen seconds. Perform on both sides.

Seated touch toes – Staying seated with both legs straight, together in front of you and feet upright. Bend from your hips rather than rounding your back. An easy way to achieve this is to look straight ahead whilst pushing your chest towards your feet. Hold this stretch for twenty seconds and keep breathing. Your hamstrings and lower back get a stretch whilst holding this position, you might also find there is a bit of tension behind your knees.

BOAT-BASED STRETCHES THAT WORK FOR ME INCLUDE:

Cross-bow stretch – This is a variation on the yoga bent knee described above, either with or without paddle. I find it is a good limber up before carrying out any cross-bow strokes.

CROSS-BOW STRETCH:

figs. 4.1-2 Cross-bow stretch. Ease into this position then relax and repeat to stretch a little further.

Arch back – When you have been sitting for a while you may find that your lower back starts to ache. One way of relieving this is to lie back in the cockpit and arch your back over the backrest or cockpit rim. Let your head fall back and try to look at the rear of your kayak (also a test of balance!).

Kiss front of cockpit – For this to be a good stretch remove your feet from the footrest and follow the directions for 'seated touch toes' above. If you keep your feet on the footrest with your knees out to the side there is not going to be a lot of stretching happening.

ARCH BACK / KISS FRONT OF COCKPIT:

figs. 4.3-4 Arch back/kiss the front of cockpit. Curl your toes back to increase the hamstring stretch.

Pull chin in / stick chin out – Most of the time when we paddle we are looking slightly down even when we are not navigating. The result of this is that our necks stiffen up. Pull your chin straight back towards your chest, it might help to push on the point of your chin with an index finger until you can feel the correct movement. Then, from the 'chin in' position, stick your chin out – extend as far forward as comfort allows and hold.

PULL CHIN IN / STICK CHIN OUT:

figs. 4.5-6 Pull chin in then stick chin out. Concentrate on the movement and muscles used.

As with all stretching, steady pressure is more beneficial than bouncing. Don't over-stretch and do pay attention to what your body is telling you. The saying 'no pain – no gain' is well out of fashion.

As with all stretching, steady pressure is more beneficial than bouncing.

For further reading on stretching see: *Stretching*, Anderson B, Pelham Books (1987)
0-7207-1351-X

4.6 MENTAL PREPARATION

Mind preparations can be as limited or as advanced as you want to make them. If you plan to paddle solo into the wide blue yonder you will have a different approach to someone who is kayaking along a sheltered stretch of coast with a group of competent friends. In his book *Alone at Sea* Hannes Lindeman wrote of constantly using 'self-talk' – "You can succeed, you are strong" – when crossing the Atlantic by kayak in 1956. Here are a few of the things that I think are important mental preparations for everyone.

- ◎ If you think you know everything there is to know about the sea, its moods and conditions, now would be a good time to put down this book, sell all of your kit and take up full body contact tiddlywinks as your sport.

- ◎ Know your ability (inability), by knowing where things start to get exciting for you; you can control your own arousal. Sometimes you will paddle outside your control parameters and be rewarded for doing so. Other times you will be in conditions well within your ability level… yet things are somehow just not right. You will know when you are 'in the groove'. Everything will be easy with plenty of time to get into position for the next part and even some time to have a look around. Unfortunately when you haven't got your head together and things are not quite right, it is a very different matter. Things start to go awry so slowly that you don't notice at first and when you do it has already become way too serious.

- ◎ Be prepared, for any eventuality. Always be aware that an accident can happen and things might not go quite according to plan. "Train hard, play easy". If like me you go out to play when conditions are bigger than you would normally go out in with others, try to do something that makes you focus all of your attention on one specific area of your performance, not using support strokes is always a good challenge.

- ◎ By navigating in poor conditions, not only do your navigation skills improve but all of your other physical and mental skills do too.

- ◎ Be flexible, change plans before you are forced into making changes you are not comfortable with. Always have a back-up plan. The what-if scenario carried out as a tabletop exercise can be a good way to focus your mind on what to do if things start to get out of hand. Depending on where you are paddling remember that the weather can change within a matter of minutes from light winds to Force 8 or more.

4.7 PLANNING

It is generally a good idea to let a shore-based contact know of your plans, whether you contact the coastguard or not is entirely up to you. Obviously if you were planning a crossing of a busy shipping channel then common sense would suggest contacting them and letting them know of your plans. Likewise if you were to plan some rescue training, letting them know beforehand might just save your day being spoilt by the arrival of a Search and Rescue helicopter and perhaps the local lifeboat as well.

When I go out I don't normally let the coastguard know where I am going or what I am doing. There are a few exceptions to this. If I am doing a night navigation exercise or rescue practice, I will speak to them and tell them what my plans are. It is common courtesy to let them know when you are off the water, although a search and rescue will not be initiated until someone reports you overdue.

One thing never to do though is to ask them what they think; the answer you will get will be a firm but definite NO! They will take the perfectly logical view that if you don't have the knowledge and experience to make the call yourself you probably shouldn't be going there. They are not advisers but they are there for you to use as a resource. Remember that the coastguard provides us with many services as well as search and rescue co-ordination. Weather forecasts are available both on VHF and by telephone. If you get to be on familiar terms with each other then generally good discussion is set up. They will tell you what the weather is doing, where they are and they will ask you what is happening where you are. This helps them build a better picture of what is actually going on and also makes them aware of what conditions we can go out in and the journeys we are able to carry out in our 'beach toys'.

If your plans are not to paddle alone then you still need to plan ahead so that you can enjoy your time on the water. A few simple things like mental or written checklists can ease the worry that you have forgotten some piece of essential equipment. This can be taken too far – an old friend used to write a list to remind him to look at all of his other lists! Obviously another way to ensure you have everything is to have a bag with all your kit already in, rather than rushing round at the last minute grabbing everything that you might use.

You will find that if you do this on a regular basis you will actually take less kit with you, and the things that you do take will be useful, with generally each item having more than one use. I always carry a comprehensive first aid kit and would advocate that you do too. Remember to include everything that you can use up to the level of your first aid training.

4.8 FEELING THE MOVES

By using your sense of feel you can begin to get an understanding of how everything relates to everything else. Does the water feel like treacle or milk? Does the kayak feel sluggish or sprightly? Does the paddle feel like a violinist's bow or a mop handle?

Kinaesthesis and proprioception are both ways you can use your body and its relation to space, time and your other body parts. By developing an awareness of how your body works in a given situation you can improve the feedback you receive from your boat, paddle and the interaction of all these things and more.

Kinaesthetic awareness is the knowledge of what is happening in close proximity to your body. The best way to think about this is to imagine the end of your kayak and how it moves in the water. Does your head hurt yet? Of course we can't know what the kayak feels like as it moves but we do know what our buttocks feel like as they move. We can feel more pressure on one side than the other. Some people's kinaesthetic awareness is so good that they know where both or either end of their kayak is at all times; the only way for you to improve this awareness is to spend a lot of time in your boat.

Proprioception is the knowledge of where your joints are in relation to each other. This is a handy skill, the greater the number of reference points you have the better your under-standing of how your actions affect other movements.

Try this exercise: Close your eyes and using your left index finger, touch the end of your nose. Most of us can do this without any problem, we know where our nose is and we also know where our finger is in relation to our nose, this is proprioception. Now have a partner sit next to you, close your eyes again and this time touch their nose with your index finger. Chances are you will have missed because we have no knowledge of where their nose is in relation to our finger, this is kinaesthesis. If you were to sit next to this person for a while, carrying out this exercise with your eyes open and closed, you would become pretty good at touching their nose. Your kinaesthetic awareness has now improved.

By closing your eyes temporarily, you can enhance your other senses including the important 'feel'. Feeling is the key to all performance paddling and a book can only offer you an insight. The only way to get better at feeling is to feel. As with all skills, this takes practice and quality practice at that.

Feeling is the key to all performance

PLATE VII *By developing awareness of kinaesthesis and proprioception you can improve intrinsic feedback.*

PLATE VIII *Perfect practice + perfect day = pretty good technique.*

5 Applied Skills

Limited space is given here to the basic handling techniques that are described in so many other books. This said however, it is important to realise that there is a difference in technique between the basic strokes and the sophisticated application of these same strokes. Skilful paddling involves **selecting** the right technique and **adapting** it to the circumstances.

Throughout this chapter I will refer often to the position and pressure on hips, knees and feet. Experimenting with this 'below decks paddling' is especially effective in a sea kayak and will lead to beneficial refinement of each of these paddle strokes and techniques.

'below decks paddling' is especially effective in a sea kayak

Analysing our techniques at their simplest level can bring greater understanding - our actions need to flow with the physical interaction between boat, blade and water. With almost all actions carried out in a sea kayak, you have momentum assisting or seemingly against you. So worthy of mention at this point is a chap called Isaac Newton, you'll probably remember him from physics at school.

NEWTON'S LAWS OF MOTION SIMPLIFIED

❶ An object moves at constant velocity unless it is acted upon by an external force.

❷ Force equals mass multiplied by acceleration.

❸ Every action has an equal and opposite reaction.

5.1 FORWARD PADDLING

Although there have been volumes written about forward paddling, it is worth spending a bit of time here discussing what constitutes good technique. Most of the time you spend in your sea kayak will be spent moving forwards, so it would seem to make sense that you try to maximise your effort and minimise the energy expended. Your forward paddling technique will change depending on what you are doing, but when there is not a strong wind blowing or other similar effect, paddle as if you were determined to impress the style judges.

As forward paddling is something that you will obviously have to do day after day and perhaps week after week, it is worth doing some sort of physical exercise, as discussed in the previous chapter, to prepare and maintain your musculoskeletal system.

Efficient and effective forward paddling needs good rotation which engages all of the big muscle groups. This works best with your knees together and slightly bent. Unfortunately, when sitting in a sea kayak, your legs will most likely be in a 'frog' position, knees apart and back supported by a comfortable backrest. These two things limit your effort to forward paddle to your best ability.

Most sea kayaks are made in such a way that you are able to brace yourself into the cockpit by using the backrest in addition to the knee or thigh braces. While this is excellent for controlling the kayak when it moves in any plane, it is not so good for best forward paddling technique. By making sure that our boat fits well but not too tightly we can have the best of both worlds, braced in the frog position for manoeuvres in the rough stuff but relaxed with knees more central most of the time.

5.2 CATCH – PULL – EXIT

The basic movement patterns of forward paddling remain very similar whatever type of paddle you use, whether wing, asymmetric or Greenland. The three key areas of catch, pull and exit of the stroke also remain fairly standard. Most sea kayakers use a stroke that starts late but is way too long.

The catch phase is perhaps the most important when you are looking at achieving efficiency. At the entry point, which you know is near to your feet, it is very important to ensure your grip is as loose as possible. If you grip tightly, it may shorten your stroke by as much as ten to twenty centimetres.

FORWARD PADDLE – LOOSE GRIP:

figs. 5.1-2 Loosening the grip on the top hand (1) to reach further forward (2) into the next catch phase. Note that in (1) the paddle has already fully exited the water with little disturbance just past the hips.

The blade should be fully immersed at the limit of your reach before you start to unwind your torso. If your arm isn't straight during the catch phase and you do use rotation well, any benefit is lost as your bent elbow straightens as you unwind your torso. This unwinding uses all the large muscle groups from your feet to your shoulders. The time to begin using your arm is when your torso starts to unwind. If you have already started pulling before the blade is fully immersed in the water, your paddle will slip, wasting the rotation you gained.

The pull phase is probably the most difficult thing within all paddlesport to get absolutely right. How you hold the paddle shaft is very important. Think of your paddle as a fragile piece of porcelain that if gripped too tightly will break in your grip. If you start your pull with a relaxed hand then gently squeeze the shaft as the pull progresses, you will find that you will be using additional muscles and will have a more powerful pull phase.

Timing of the exit of the blade from the water is important. If left too late, you will be lifting water behind you. This pulls the rear of the kayak down into the water and doesn't make a lot of sense. Aim for the blade to be clipped out by your hips.

By using a cranked paddle shaft (modified or double torque) you will go some way to improving the catch phase, as long as you remember to exit early the advantage will be clear.

5.3 REVERSE PADDLING

When paddling backwards you should be aiming to 'rewind' your forward stroke. Plant near your hips and push through towards the bow.

Steering when going backwards can be challenging but if you aim to make the last part of your stroke the steering component things will start to become easier. By driving the blade towards your feet at the end of the stroke you are performing the equivalent of a stern draw. This should ensure you at least go in some sort of straight line. To reverse sweep effectively when going backwards is difficult and normally you will have to do two or three sweeps to start a turn. Unfortunately by the time the kayak responds you will have oversteered and will have to start the reverse sweep thing on the other side. A reverse sweep has to be carried out faster than the reverse paddle stroke for it to be effective.

Looking over your shoulder every stroke or second stroke is not required. If you have looked and there is nothing behind you for a bit, why look again? Obviously if there is something fairly close you will want to glance to see where you are in relation to it.

5.4 SWEEP STROKES

When you apply the paddle at a distance from your body you are initiating a turning moment; the further away the point of leverage is from your body the more efficient the resulting turn will be. This is a fairly elementary statement but not often observed.

EXTENDED PADDLE POSITION:

fig. 5.3 Extended paddle position.

fig. 5.4 Forward sweep broken down into segments.

❶ *From the bow to the end of the first segment the bow moves away from the paddle.*

❷ *From the end of the first segment to the end of the second segment the kayak moves forwards.*

❸ *From the end of the second segment to the stern has little or no effect on turning. It does however have an effect on the stability of your shoulder joint.*

Sliding your hands along the paddle shaft to extend your reach brings obvious rewards, however if you are using crank shaft paddles, moving your hand position is often undesirable. Alternatively you may increase your effective turning moment by committing to the paddle by leaning and also ensuring that your arms are fully extended into the sweep.

When looking at the arc of the paddle through the water we have to modify the path it takes or our advantage will be lost to inefficiency, instability and discomfort. In an ideal world the paddle would stay in one spot and the kayak would rotate around it. Unfortunately this will never happen, as your paddle blade will certainly not have a bigger surface area than your kayak. If we try to imagine the forces between kayak and sea and the limitations of our bodily movements then we can begin to develop a more efficient method.

FORWARD SWEEP:

figs. 5.5-7 Forward sweep through all three segments. Stern segment least effective.

As an exercise try the three segments of the sweep individually. Choose calm water with a static object close by (as a point of reference), point the bow at it and then perform each segment in turn. An alternative would be to have someone video you so that you can get feedback as to how your kayak moves.

For very many motor skills the head leads the movement, sea kayaking is no different. If you pre-rotate your head and shoulders to face your intended direction of travel you can reach further towards the bow. This allows you to unwind your torso using the largest muscle groups as you drive the kayak through the turn with your feet.

So, back to Newton's third law. When you are pressing or driving your feet where are you actually pushing towards? With your knees in the frog position, if you apply your foot on the outside of the turn to the centre of the kayak and brace off it, your turning moment will benefit (compare this to the effect of bringing your feet together when in the knees up position for efficient forward paddling).

Obviously this is easy to achieve with a bulkhead footrest but a similar effect can be felt when using pedal footrests. With a bulkhead it is most simple to move your outside foot across towards the centre line of the boat and push there. With pedal footrests, instead of pressing with the balls of your feet you can use the big toe side and push off the inside edge of the footrest.

What would be the result if you were to push on the side of the kayak with your little toe on the inside of the turn? Experimenting with the way you think about the forces on your knees, feet, buttocks, back and hips (all the points of contact through which forces are transmitted to and from your boat and body) will bring an added dimension to all your strokes. Move around in your kayak, adjust your technique to your own boat, seat, knee area and footrest and let the subtle effects take their course.

fig. 5.8 The crest of a wave presents an opportunity to make quick changes of direction.

This is all very well on flat water but what happens when you paddle in more challenging conditions? Moving up and down doesn't cause any particular problems for turning; however, it does force you to act accordingly. If you time your application of the sweep at the wave crest then your turn will be executed a lot easier. Make sure the blade is fully immersed in the water before the kayak reaches the peak of the wave and that the sweep has just started. This means that the kayak will already be turning when most of it is out of the water.

In bigger seas the quickest way to turn is to be paddling toward the crest and apply a sweep as above with maximum power on the blade as your feet cross the top of the wave. If you push your feet towards the intended direction then the result will be the start of a very dynamic turn. For most sea kayaks it is possible to turn at least 90° with this one stroke alone, due in part to there being not a lot of the boat in the water. If there is a decent wind blowing towards you at the same time then it will tend to push you around as well.

If you are planning to turn and face the other direction, after the forward sweep immediately lean to the inside of the turn and prepare to execute a reverse sweep/crunch with the kayak as far onto its edge as you will allow it to go.

REVERSE SWEEP:

figs. 5.9-11 Effective reverse sweep through two segments.

5.5 REVERSE SWEEP/CRUNCH

When you do a reverse sweep, the best starting position is at the rear of the kayak. Trunk rotation allows your blade to enter the water closer to the stern, however, if you reach behind your normal operating area without rotation, you are putting your shoulder at risk.

A good idea is to edge as far as you are able until the kayak is off balance, then when you plant the blade you can transfer some weight to the paddle. As the live blade is now moving away from the rear of the kayak, and into a low brace position, you can lean to this side much more than edging alone would allow. What is actually happening here is that you have released more of the keel from the water.

This in turn allows you to use your leg and stomach muscles to pull the boat through the turn. The movement is not dissimilar to a regular 'crunch' that you would perform in a gym. If you imagine pulling your knees towards your chest while they are still engaged below the deck then that is a good starting place.

Again look at the various segments that make up the arc of the paddle as it travels through the water. You will see that the first and second components are the more dynamic whilst the last, or front part, is the least effective. Throughout the stroke maintain an edge that reflects your ability and ensure that your blade placement is as far from the centre line of the kayak as possible.

5.6 CROSS-BOW JAB

This 'jab' deflects the track of your kayak and is used to initiate a turn. By performing a momentary cross-bow rudder on the inside of the turn, you will have pre-rotated far enough to allow a powerful dynamic sweep to take place. This can be awkward to achieve at first but it is definitely worth persevering with. If this initiation is combined with 'edge change' below, the change of direction can be quite dramatic.

5.7 EDGE CHANGE (inside to outside)

Some kayaks, especially those with a true chined hull and a few of the lower volume designs which have a relatively deep bow, behave slightly differently to the majority and for these it is necessary to edge into the turn to start the edge release. This inside edge phase is only momentary at the start of the sweep with transfer to the outside edge happening immediately the bow starts to come round.

5.8 STATIC DRAW (classic & sculling)

Different kayaks need to be edged in different ways for the draw to work most effectively. The effect you are trying to achieve is the kayak sliding over the water and therefore the underwater hull shape is important. A deep vee section on a hull (eg. Sirius, Qajariaq, Greenlander) will draw best if edged slightly towards the direction of travel whereas a flatter hull (eg. Capella, Aquanaut, Romany) performs better either flat or edged slightly away from the draw side. As with all twiddly strokes this works best if your paddle is nearer vertical than horizontal.

5.9 DRAW ON THE MOVE

A very dynamic stroke when carried out in a sea kayak. The intention is to move the kayak towards the side the paddle is placed as quickly as possible in order that forward paddling can continue immediately afterwards. This is of use when manoeuvring whilst rockhopping, last minute collision avoidance and anywhere that sudden and immediate sideways movement is required.

With the kayak travelling at its cruising speed, lean a long way to the side you intend drawing towards, plant your blade at right angles to your kayak about 1.5m from the gunwale and then carry out a strong pull with the leading edge of the live blade just 'open'. Try to use your hips to make this move happen, after the plant and as you start to pull, use all of your lower torso muscles to 'bump your bum' to the side you are moving towards. The movement is very like a dance called 'The Bump' which I have a vague recollection of! As you come close to finishing the pull, flatten your kayak off so that you return to the upright position.

fig. 5.12 Draw on the move. Leaning overboard sets up the 'bump' whilst edging to keep the boat flat (in a round bilged kayak like this one).

5.10 HANGING DRAW

This is a very useful, graceful stroke. Used for side-slipping your kayak over a longer distance than the previous draw. Useful when coming alongside a harbour or slipway and paddling alongside another person; if your courses will most likely result in a collision, one or both can draw away. When correctly applied there is little appreciable drop in momentum unless used as a final stroke for landing.

fig. 5.13 *Paddle position for hanging draw.*

Easy to apply once mastered, but difficult to master. The key to getting the whole thing working is to know where the pivot point of your kayak is when travelling forwards.

The working blade should be placed in the water parallel to the boat (this varies depending on boat and body) at your hips, in the neutral position. Open the drive face gradually so that the water pressure acts to pull your arm away from the kayak. If you resist this lateral displacement your kayak will slip towards the side of the paddle. Your feet should be quite neutral throughout this stroke although your foot on the side away from the paddle will be pushing on the footrest due mainly to your body rotation.

5.11 BOW DRAW

Quite simply a draw stroke done towards the front of your kayak. Useful for starting a turn, which is then turned into a power stroke. If you use your feet as the starting point for this you will achieve best results. Pre-rotate your body towards the side you are going to draw. With a bent arm plant the blade in the water about one metre from your feet ensuring the drive face is angled towards the kayak. Then, using the rotation, unwind your body and finish by pulling the blade towards the kayak with your arm.

figs. 5.14-15 *Bow draw sequence. The more you are able to pre-rotate your shoulders (14) the more efficient your draw (15).*

5.12 FUTURE WATER

Originally a concept borrowed from squirt boating, within sea kayaking 'future water' relates to the interaction between water and paddle blade.

Your paddle is the lever with which you effect any change of direction. In order that it can work as an effective point of leverage, it has to be biting into future water. When turning, in still water, using the strokes below (bow rudder and cross-bow rudder) there comes a point when the water the working blade is slicing through equalises pressure on the back and front of the blade if you keep the angle between blade and boat constant. This effectively slows any turn and you have to do something in order that your equipment can work for you to maintain the effectiveness of the turn. As you slow, the relative angle of blade to kayak has to increase to allow pressure to stay higher on the power face. This changing angle or 'changle' is paramount if best use is to be made of the momentum you and your boat have gathered.

This changing angle or 'changle' is paramount...

5.13 BOW RUDDER

A well-executed bow rudder in a sea kayak is a delight to use and delightful to watch. It does require good timing, edge control and blade placement to make it work, but as discussed earlier, a sea kayak has mass in its favour – it is possible to turn 180° and still have a bit of momentum.

The first part of the turn is to make the break from forward travel, this can be done a number of ways, for example:

Sweep initiation – remember you are travelling at the same speed as the kayak, so when you apply a sweep stroke at the front of the kayak it will have to be a fast and dynamic stroke if there is to be any effect on the change of direction. A partial sweep in the front segment applies maximum effect quickly and leads more swiftly into the rudder stroke. Sometimes you might have to do several sweeps to get the bow to break away.

Stern draw initiation – often a better option is to apply a bit of a stern draw before initiating the edge. This can be added to the end of your last forward paddle stroke and works off your forward momentum (rather than being impeded by it).

After your kayak has started to turn, edge towards the outside of the turn while ensuring your body weight is forwards. Aim to get your whole paddle as perpendicular as possible with the elbow on the inside of the turn held close to the top of your pelvis. Ideally your top hand should be around the position of your forehead and the gap between your arms being a window to look through or your top arm being a bar to look over. This compact position allows the blade to be fully immersed in the water with minimal risk to your shoulders. Your foot that is on the outside of the turn has to work hard at pushing on the footrest, this ensures your whole body is being used. The knee on the inside of the turn is hooked under the deck and that foot presses hard on the side of the kayak. With the live blade in the water in a neutral position, gently open the drive face towards the direction of travel. As long as the live blade is biting into future water all the time, your turn will continue until momentum stops. See chapter on tidal paddling for variation.

fig. 5.16 Flexibility is key in maintaining your outside edge whilst planting the paddle as vertical as possible.

fig. 5.17 Bringing larger muscle groups into play, the cross-bow maximises the benefits of leverage.

5.14 CROSS-BOW RUDDER

A few years ago this was seen as a show-off stroke. It has now gained popularity amongst many sea kayakers for several reasons.

- ◎ The water that gathers on your upper blade does not drip off and land on the only exposed piece of flesh, which is normally the back of your neck.

- ◎ The stability of your shoulder joint when performing the stroke.

- ◎ By rotating to get into position you are already setting the edge and pushing on the footrest with the correct foot.

Bring your kayak to its cruising speed and initiate the turn by using a sharp first segment sweep. When the sweep has finished, bring this 'live' blade all the way across the front of the kayak until it is above the water on the inside of the turn. If you are holding the shaft the same way as you were for the sweep, the angle is already set for you. Gently drop the blade into the water in the neutral position where there is least resistance and no turning effect. Now if you gradually open the drive face to the direction of travel by rolling your wrists away from you, the blade will start biting into future water. If you now edge away from the paddle side even more, you will find that you will also be able to balance your weight against the pull on the paddle. Hold onto this position for as long as you want the turn to continue or until there is no momentum left.

To apply the cross-bow rudder you may choose to rotate even further, keeping your wrists in a similar position to when you finished the sweep. If you were to drop the live blade into the water at this extended position it would not do your joints any favours. So roll your wrists towards you, setting the blade angle nearer to neutral. Extra torso rotation allows you to make use of your whole body to make the turn. As the kayak slows, adjust the blade to grip future water and consider finishing with a cross-bow draw to gain an extra few degrees of turn.

When you use a cross-bow rudder you engage all of your body from your feet to your fingers, in addition the larger muscle groups are working for you to produce the turn. The standard bow rudder limits how much of your body is working when turning a sea kayak – even with your elbow locked to your waist it is the smaller, unstable muscles of your shoulder that are doing much of the work.

I know a few people who have dislocated a shoulder when performing a bow rudder, but have never heard of anyone who has done so with one of the cross-bow flavour. However, when learning the cross-bow rudder there is a much greater chance of a capsize.

HIGH ANGLE / DYNAMIC STERN RUDDER:

figs. 5.18-19 Keeping the top hand high (18) enables the whole blade to be active without leaning back or dropping the lower hand into the water (19).

5.15 STERN RUDDER

Principally a steering stroke, but performed well it can become a turning stroke in its own right when used with a good amount of edge. Used when travelling with a following sea and steering into tight places such as narrow cave entrances.

There are two positions for stern rudder and two schools of thought:

Low angle – If you adopt the 'old school' low paddle angle method, you will find that your trailing hand has to be in the water to ensure the rear blade is completely submerged. Also with this technique you will probably be leaning back which locks your spine, inhibiting rotation and puts more weight towards the stern of the kayak. This 'trim' affects the whole steering ability of you and your kayak combination. The stern is more likely to lock onto its track and continue to run towards where it was pointing.

High angle – Much better is the dynamic rudder position. This is when your front hand is around shoulder height, rear hand just above the water, body in the upright to slightly forward position but rotated to the paddle side. This position allows you to use more of your body to torque the kayak through the turns.

With the kayak moving forwards at a reasonable speed, rotate towards the side the rudder is going to be used. Aim to plant the blade in the neutral position (blade parallel to the direction of movement) about 30cm from the kayak with your trailing arm behind you. Try to keep the elbow of your trailing arm close to, or touching the top of your pelvis. To turn your kayak towards the side the paddle is on, just move your front hand towards the kayak, to turn away push your front hand away. With your lower arm locked against your pelvis the shoulder is well protected.

Another way to work the rudder blade is to rotate it around the axis of the paddle shaft. Rolling your wrists away (wrist higher than knuckles) from you increases pressure on the non-drive face and decreases pressure on the drive face closest to the boat. This 'wing' effect forces the paddle toward the boat. Holding the paddle in place and resisting this force transmits this force through to the stern of the boat pushing it in a direction away from the paddle. Rolling your wrists towards (wrist lower than knuckles) you opens the drive face to the flow, increasing the pressure on this face and decreasing pressure on the non-drive face, the result is a force drawing the blade away from the boat. As you are holding your paddle with your elbow firmly locked to your pelvis, this force is transmitted to the boat, drawing the stern in the direction of the paddle.

5.16 STERN DRAW

Rather similar to the variation on the stern rudder where the kayak turns toward the paddle side. Performed in a similar manner, the aim is to have the back of the kayak draw towards the paddle rather than allowing the bow to lead the way.

You already know of the difficulties of applying an effective forward sweep whilst moving. The stern draw acts on the rear of the kayak. This is most commonly the part of the kayak that resists turning and if you are able to release the boat from its track, it will start to skid into a turn. The stern draw can be a good initiation stroke for turning sequences and lends itself to the initiation of some of the other more static strokes carried out towards the front of the kayak. Normally a short sharp stroke works better than a lingering one.

STERN DRAW:

Your paddle will be in the dynamic rudder position, with the power face just open. Drop the rear blade into the water about 30cm from the gunwale and pull towards the kayak, removing it from the water before it trips you up. Push with your foot on the blade side to work the boat.

fig. 5.20 Similar to the dynamic stern rudder, you can blend this stroke in neatly from a forward power or sweep stroke.

5.17 CROSS-BOW DRAW

See under cross-bow rudder for the basic set-up and positioning. Make sure your last stroke is on the same side you intend to draw towards, this ensures that minimum turning effect is induced. As with any other draw, your paddle should be perpendicular to your hips in a neutral position. This allows both hands to be held over the side of the kayak and any drips fall into the water and not down your neck.

WOULD YOU LIKE SALT WITH THAT SIR?

Brian Wilson in his book *Blazing Paddles*[†], talks about being able to salt his meal just by rubbing his eyebrows. If your face and forehead are constantly getting showered with salt water, the residue left after the water has evaporated mixes with your sweat and runs into your eyes. This saturate salt solution always seems to arrive at just the wrong time and really stings.

† Brian Wilson, *Blazing Paddles, a Scottish Coastal Odyssey*
Wildland Press (1998)

5.18 LOW BRACE TURN

For a long time coaches have been using a series of progressions to get students to develop a balanced, edged low brace turn. Unfortunately, with an ingraining of this method many of these students have since become coaches and teach the low brace turn as an edged turn with the back face of the paddle just above the water as an end result rather than a means to an end.

A low brace turn slows the kayak and is done with your body leaning well into the turn, supported on the paddle and by centrifugal force, and held until the angle of turn is achieved or momentum stops. Used whenever a high-speed turn is required but loss of momentum is not an issue (eg. breaking out of the current or manoeuvring for a rescue).

figs. 5.21-22 Keeping the top hand high (21) enables the whole blade to be active without leaning back or dropping the lower hand into the water (22).

Have the kayak up to its running speed, do the first segment of the forward sweep to start the turn, rotate your shoulders well towards the inside of the turn and look to where you want to go. Make sure your body weight is forward and well towards the inside of the turn. Place the live blade on the surface of the water in the climbing attitude as far from the centre line of the kayak as you can reach. If you put the blade on the water just behind your hips with your body rotated, there is minimal danger to your shoulder joint. When your momentum has slowed and the blade is just about to sink, slice the live blade through the water towards the stern and then immediately convert this into a reverse sweep crunch.

5.19 COLORADO HOOK

During the first kayak descent of the Colorado River (when whitewater kayaks were four metres or longer) someone found that to get into an eddy a cross-bow rudder was more effective. The added instability forced the paddler to rely on a reverse sweep transition into a low brace then paddle up the eddy into safety – and so became the Colorado Hook.

As a method for turning a sea kayak it is pretty good, but it's excellent for developing total awareness of your body and boat. Every component of the stroke leads from the last and links to the next. For the whole sequence to flow the blade must slice through the water.

figs. 5.23-25 From a forward sweep into a cross-bow rudder (23), reverse sweep (24), bow draw (25).

To turn to the left, the sequence is: forward momentum, dynamic first segment sweep on right, cross-bow rudder on left held until momentum has ceased or kayak has turned sufficiently, drop upper blade on left into water and reverse sweep until around 50cm from bow, roll wrists backwards until blade flops onto drive face then bow draw until close to the kayak, turning this finally into a forward power stroke. Apart from the initial sweep, every other part of this stroke sequence is performed on the inside of the turn.

You will find that the turn can be executed more efficiently if you use your feet to drive the kayak through the turn on the cross-bow part, then edging beyond your normal limit will allow the bow to come around further before applying the bow draw. If you practise this combination stroke and try to get a feel of what is going on below your spraydeck, you will gain an insight into the use of your legs for most of the other skills you perform.

5.20 HIGH WIND TURN

As with the Colorado Hook, this requires practice so that it can be applied when required. Sometimes you will find yourself in a situation where you are facing downwind and no amount of sweeping will turn the bow of your kayak into the wind. Hopefully you will have read this section before you are heading off into the great blue yonder!

If you are wanting to turn to the left: reverse paddle into the wind applying full power, carry out one or two first segment reverse sweep/crunch strokes on your left to start the direction change. When this change happens, be ready to drop your right shoulder towards the water with your right paddle blade on the surface about 50cm from the front of the kayak and with your right arm almost straight. If you now hold this position until you have almost come to a standstill, the kayak will be turning all the while. Now, perform a forward sweep on this side as you lift yourself from the water, (the first two segments work best) and immediately this is finished a reverse sweep/crunch on the left side is applied. If you have not turned 180° then carry out the forward sweep – reverse sweep/crunch sequence until you are completely round.

figs. 5.26-29 From backward power with a couple of reverse sweep/crunches on the left, then into a forward brace position (26), holding the brace into a continued turn (27) converting this into a forward sweep (28-29) and finishing with a reverse sweep/ crunch on the left if required. Photos: Morag Brown.

5.21 BETTER EDGING

Our kayaks, we know from the chapter on boat dynamics, turn more easily if put onto an edge. What we have to try to do is to use this most effectively, with minimum energy expenditure and maximum effect.

Consider weighting one buttock more than the other when we are setting an edge so the opposite knee becomes our 'fine tuning' device. This is quite a departure from the 'lift the knee' school of inducing edge – although they quite often amount to the same thing, the real difference is the effectiveness of the concept – the idea of weighting one buttock is much easier to understand for most paddlers. The result is that because the edge is initiated by a body-weight shift then there is likely to be less fatigue when compared to bracing a knee against the kayak to maintain an edge. In addition fewer muscles are being employed to keep the kayak on edge so more can be used for turning the kayak.

5.22 LAUNCH & LAND

There are as many different ways to launch or land as you can imagine. There are, however, a few basic rules to make things a bit easier for you and might prolong your equipment life.

- ◎ Use as many helpers as you have available to manoeuvre your kayak from the roof, trailer or rack.

- ◎ Using these same folk, take good hold of the boat at or near its strong points. Carrying this way will save not just your back but also those of your companions and might just save your boat from dropping and being damaged.

- ◎ Use a trolley to transport the boat to the water when you have no helpers.

fig. 5.30 If you have a high vehicle then it might be worthwhile considering the Kari-Tek roof-rack system. This semi-dismountable rack lowers your kayak(s) to around one metre from the ground and reduces the chance of back injury.

A really good way to damage your nice paddle is to sit on it when getting into or out of your kayak. I would recommend, as would paddle manufacturers, not to use your paddle for this. So what other options are available?

- ◎ Have your boat floating.

- ◎ Straddle it when you can.

- ◎ Keep your paddle close, perhaps held under the deck elastics.

- ◎ Lie back to get your body weight low.

- ◎ Keep your feet in the water for added stability.

- ◎ If you are coming from above ensure your weight is centred on the kayak with your feet in the cockpit.

- ◎ Practise as many different scenarios for launching and landing as possible.

Sometimes the only way to get afloat is to face up to the fact that you are going to have to get into the water, swim with your kayak then perform some sort of circus trick in order to get into the cockpit. There are many ways to do this but all require practice until there is no hesitation. The rescue chapter looks into some methods of self-rescue.

SEAL LAUNCH & LAND – This can be a fun way to get onto, and off the water. It is however a guaranteed way to take a shaving from the bottom of your kayak. Plastic survives well but does start to get hairy with just a few launches. Composite kayaks make noises that sound as if it is being torn apart, great holes being punched in it and you can just imagine the credit card bill for the repairs when it comes through your letterbox.

Aim to have the kayak in a position that will allow you to slide into the water. Having attached your spraydeck and holding your paddle in one hand, time your push with the other hand so that your boat slides from the rock and plunges into the water as the oncoming waves are at their highest point. This technique relies on there being enough water below your kayak when you try to float it and also you must consider the 'what if' scenario. Picture yourself in your kayak having attempted a seal launch from a marginal place, the kayak has not cleared the rock and the swell has passed. Your bow is now buried deep in the water resting on some rocks with the stern a long way above your head. If you are lucky the next swell will lift your kayak and you will be able to finish your launch. If this does not happen then you will probably have to get out and try to salvage your gear. Obviously it is much better to use one of the other methods if at all possible, and keep this as a last resort.

fig. 5.31 *Grey seals on Mingulay.*

PLATE IX *Rescue bay door on military SH-3 Sea King helicopter.*
©iStockphoto.com / Mike Pettifer

6 Safety & Rescue

Rescues carried out at sea have the same inherent problems as those on whitewater. They have the added complication of there being no bank-side access and there is huge potential for things to go 'Big Wrong'. However, the theory of all rescue scenarios remains the same whether it is on the sea, on whitewater or inside a collapsing building.

PROTECT ➤ ❶ YOURSELF | ❷ THE REMAINING GROUP MEMBERS | ❸ THE VICTIM

In this order, and continually re-evaluate the risks involved.

Rescues are an important skill for a competent kayaker, whether it is you who is rescuing or being rescued doesn't matter. What matters is the way these rescues are carried out, the speed at which the swimmer is put back into their boat and the immediate after-effects of the situation. The swimmer must remain in contact with their kayak and paddle until the rescuer arrives; what happens after that is almost entirely up to the rescuer. The fastest rescue does not involve the victim moving around their kayak onto the rescuer's, but just keeping hold of their boat. When moving around in the water always keep hold of the deck lines. If there was a best location to be, it would be at the front of your kayak as this is where the rescuer will arrive and you can hand over your kayak whilst you transfer onto the rescuer's. It almost goes without saying that by practising a variety of rescues in different controlled conditions your armoury will be increased, ensuring you are far more capable than if you only ever tried one type of rescue.

IMPORTANT INFORMATION FOR ALL RESCUERS

Ascertain the mental state of the swimmer. Until they prove otherwise by appearing calm and answering questions logically, assume that they will make a grab for you and try to climb onto your kayak. Assume that every victim is trying to get you into the water alongside them.

If you can't do it without compromising yourself, don't do it. It is better to have one person in dire straits than two. Only after you have ensured that they are calm and in control should you make contact.

Handle with Care! Slide – don't lift! A fully laden sea kayak can weigh 200kg before it has any water in the cockpit. Don't bend to the side. Keep your spine in line when viewed from behind, it is a very strong structure in this position but weak as soon as there is any lateral deflection.

Use the victim to help if at all possible. Ensure they hold onto their kayak and paddle, talk to them, give them instructions, even cajole or bully them, whatever it takes to make the rescue run smoothly.

The rescuer has absolute control. The rescuer commands respect from the victim. The swimmer must listen and react to instructions as soon as they are given, even anticipating what the rescuer might ask them to do.

6.1 SELF RESCUE

With the exception of a 'bombproof' roll, most of these fall into the party tricks category, sometimes useful to convince yourself that you will be all right no matter what happens. Unfortunately the conditions that managed to put you into the water in the first place will still be there when you are back in your kayak with the added inconvenience of having the cockpit area full of water. As with any other rescue type scenario, practising in different sea conditions will let you make an informed choice as to which method works for you when you need it.

6.2 ROLL

When it comes to rolling a sea kayak there is little difference from other craft. Things just need to happen more slowly. Due to the overall volume of the kayak and also the buoyancy near the ends, a typical sea kayak will tend to lie on its side rather than invert completely. You can go some way to reducing this problem by ensuring you tuck your chin into your chest and have your head as close to the front deck as you can get it.

All too often when you capsize and don't go all the way over you will be on your 'wrong' side, if you are able to roll on both sides there is not a problem. If you have a lot of buoyancy on your upper body due to trapped air in your paddling top or whatever, there is a high chance that when you try to set up for a roll the kayak will start to come up on the 'wrong' side again. This is one time that I can think of when a sculling support would be useful. By sculling you are moving your kayak under the water to get it into a roll set up position.

SCREW ROLL:

figs. 6.1–5 Screw roll.
An alternative finish involving ending the roll on a reverse low brace scull can be beneficial when rolling a laden sea kayak. This allows greater stability when you are back upright.

6.3   RE-ENTER AND ROLL

Probably the most used and secure method of performing a self-rescue. It does take practice however and this should include difficult water. Start in the water beside your upturned kayak. Hold your paddle and the part of the cockpit nearest you in your left hand. Lie back in the water and start to put your feet into the cockpit, as you do this move the kayak onto its side. Now hold the cockpit with a hand on either side and pull your buttocks all the way into the seat. You will invert completely at this point. Making sure you are locked into the thigh braces and footrest, perform a slow roll. There will be a substantial amount of water in the cockpit that will affect your stability, so retreat to somewhere you are able to pump out your kayak and then replace your spraydeck.

RE-ENTER AND ROLL:

figs. 6.6-10   Re-enter and roll. Ensure you are completely in the cockpit before attempting to roll.

6.4   CLAMBER ON BACK DECK

Getting from the water onto the back deck of your kayak without assistance may be possible. Keep close to the cockpit area where the kayak is widest. Push yourself out of the water and onto the back deck in one move. This is best performed by sinking yourself into the water then pull down and kick at the same time, push up until you can lie upon the rear deck. By keeping your weight low and wide this is a reasonably stable position and it should now be possible for you to shuffle forward until you can sit down into the seat. When you are in the seat bring your legs in one at a time.

figs. 6.11–14 Clamber on back deck. This method obviously requires good balance.

fig. 6.15 Foam paddle float, easier to use but bulkier to store. © Northwater.com

6.5 PADDLE FLOAT

Paddle float self-rescue seems like a good idea and it works in calm conditions. But those who can perform this trick in rough water are often able to clamber on the back deck with better balance. Begin by righting your kayak. Place the paddle float over one blade, if it's inflatable blow it up. Place the paddle across the back deck behind the cockpit and holding it down, push yourself out of the water until you are lying face down on the paddle and deck. You should be far enough back on the deck to slide your feet into the cockpit whilst you remain face down. Once in the cockpit (as far as you can) twist around until you are sitting upright. Remove the paddle float and replace it where it is available for your next use.

figs. 6.16–19 Using a paddle float. Keep your weight low for as long as possible.

fig. 6.20 Re-enter and roll with paddle float. This is also a good method of improving your 're-enter and roll' in more challenging conditions.

6.6 SOLO RESCUES

By definition, these rescues involve one rescuer in addition to the capsized victim; normally this would take the form of an X rescue* or similar (see Ultimate Rescue overleaf).

6.7 ESKIMO RESCUES

Considered the second line of defence after a roll but before a wet exit. The basic Eskimo rescue involves holding your breath, staying in your upturned kayak, attracting attention by banging loudly on the hull, waving your arms about, hoping that your paddling buddies will manage to manoeuvre their kayaks close enough to you to let you get hold of some part of their kayak, paddle or body. Now imagine this if you are paddling in breaking seas or a tide race… it's not always a good option.

When inverted, bang loudly on the hull of your kayak, then with your thumbs pointing towards the hull, sweep your hands along the sides of the kayak in a wide arc. Open your eyes to see your rescuer arriving from one or other side. Wait until you feel a bump from their kayak hitting yours. You should now be very close to making contact with your hand. When you have hold of the rescuer's kayak, pull down on it and using a hip flick right yourself, making sure that you keep hold of your rescuer's boat. If the rescuer approaches the upturned kayak at an angle, there is a much larger target for you to get hold of. In addition the rescuer doesn't have to be super accurate with positioning their kayak.

ESKIMO RESCUE:

21　　*22*

figs. 6.21-22　End of kayak presentation followed by execution of rescue. See how John's hands are turned to maximise chance of contact.

* **X rescue**, the old standard. The upturned kayak is pulled onto the rescuer's kayak until the balance point is reached, then with a see-saw motion the water is emptied from the kayak.

THREE APPROACHES:

Bow-to-bow – the rescuer approaches from the front and when he reaches your bow he holds onto it. This puts his bow into a position where you are easily able to get hold of it. Pull up as the other methods.

End of kayak presentation – simplest to perform but not the easiest to line up. The bow of the rescuer's kayak comes in at an angle from the front, ensuring this makes contact with your boat before reaching your hands. The bump alerts you.

Paddle presentation – rescuer's kayak comes alongside, his paddle is put over your upturned hull and your hand (from between the kayaks) is guided onto the paddle shaft. Your rescuer can stabilise you as you pull yourself out of the water.

Perhaps a good way to look at performing an Eskimo rescue would be to consider the 'what if' scenario. Imagine you are approaching from the bow; you as the rescuer have set yourself up for the bow-to-bow method and you are almost there, a wave knocks your hand from the bow just as you are about to hold it. If you had angled your kayak more towards the upturned hull your bow would hit just about the right place for a bow rescue to happen. If you miss this place then your momentum will carry you along the side of the upturned kayak and your paddle can be brought across into position for the paddle rescue.

6.8 ULTIMATE RESCUE

Approach the bow of the upturned kayak and put your paddle in a restraint when you have a firm grip on the boat. Make sure you have both hands on the boat with the one nearest some way along the keel. This lets you use the buoyancy of this boat for support as you get

ULTIMATE RESCUE:

figs. 6.23-27 Ultimate rescue. This method of rescue places little stress on the rescuer's body but does require practice.

fig. 6.28 *Using the crook of his arm the rescuer empties the kayak. With the victim on the bow it is possible to monitor their condition more easily.*

your other hand into position on the bow. Using both hands turn the kayak up the right way, then still holding onto the toggle or end, lean away from the boat you are rescuing until your kayak is completely on its side, whilst pulling the kayak onto your own. This movement will turn the boat you are rescuing so that the water can drain from the cockpit. (Another option is to slide the kayak onto your own until you reach the front hatch. Turn it upside down into the crook of your arm which is closest to the cockpit of the rescued kayak). When the water has drained turn the kayak up the right way as you sit back into the upright position. Pass the bow under your armpit until you reach the front of the cockpit. Keeping your head low, hold onto the deck lines on either side of the boat and have the centre line of the victim's kayak in line with your armpit, with your kayak on edge. Using your stomach muscles perform a crunch by pulling your knees towards your chest, this ensures both kayaks stay close together. In this position you will be able to help the victim if required and then assist with refitting their spraydeck.

METHODS OF GETTING BACK IN:

Push up re-entry – push up near the cockpit with a kayak on either side. If you let your body sink into the water first you will allow the buoyancy to help your lift as it tries to get to the surface. When your arms are straight, swivel until you can sit in your own cockpit. Then it is just a case of getting your feet in and refitting your spraydeck.

Lie back re-entry – lie back between your own and your rescuer's boat facing towards them. Hook an arm and a leg over each kayak, then by levering with your arms and legs pull the kayaks together below you. Sit up and get your legs into the cockpit. This method is not very easy and poses the risk of the kayaks colliding if there is any wave movement whatsoever.

figs. 6.29-31
Lie–back
re-entry.

LIE-BACK RE-ENTRY:

Leg over from the outside – face the rear of your kayak, holding on behind your cockpit, hook your leg which is nearest the kayak into the cockpit. If you now straighten your leg as you pull up with your arms you will find that you are out of the water and almost completely in the kayak. Simply slide your other leg in, twist around and replace your spraydeck.

figs. 6.32-34
Leg over
re-entry.
This method
uses large
muscles.

LEG OVER RE-ENTRY:

Scoop re-entry (assisting injured paddler) – have the injured paddler hold onto their kayak, which you put onto its side with the cockpit away from you. Assist the victim to get their legs and buttocks into the cockpit (or turn so that their back is facing the cockpit and ma-noeuvre the buttocks into the seat). Grasp the buoyancy aid and pull towards you, at the same time pushing their kayak down into the water. The kayak will bob back up in the water and help you lift. Remember to hold onto the victim when you have them upright.

figs. 6.35-37
Scoop
re-entry.

SCOOP RE-ENTRY:

6.9 GROUP RESCUES

Used where a weaker person has already started carrying out the rescue but is not quite managing, with support for the rescuer or victim. For example, where the victim and rescuer are being swept onto rocks or other inhospitable coastline. In this case a towed rescue works well, assuming some group member has a tow system.

Consider how you would deal with a situation where a group member was unable to paddle due to an accident or illness. There are many models you can look at to help you deal with any incident. The one below is how I approach a developing situation:

C — **Collect** your thoughts

A — **Assess** the complete situation and formulate a plan with back-up

M — **Manage** yourself first, the rest of the group, then the casualty

E — **Execute** plan A

R — **Review** the incident in context and as a whole

A — **Assess** plan A's effectiveness and modify it given the evolving situation

Although presented here as a list, this could easily be drawn as a flow chart or even a circle. I believe it is important to see it as a continuum with no end and no predetermined starting point. The reason for this is that you should be assessing the situation and managing everyone at all times whether there is an incident or not and whether you are the group leader or not. I like to use CAMERA because if it were possible to film the whole event from before it became an incident until after everyone was home safe there would be a great many lessons to be learnt from it.

The more complex the environment, the more difficult the rescue. There may be no landing sites available such as when you are alongside cliffs. You could be forced offshore in a strong tidal race or unfavourable wind. You could even be in a busy shipping area and almost completely invisible to their radar.

"For your rescues to work they require to be practised on a regular basis in all conditions"

fig. 6.38
Group
assisted
rescue.

fig. 6.39
Towed
rescue.

6.10 TOWING

The reasons for having to tow someone are boundless as are the methods of towing; it could be anything from tiredness, illness, injury or holding position off a steep coastline during a rescue, but you may well be required to tow someone for a considerable period of time at some point.

When you make the decision to tow, the chances are that you will already be tired and things are not going according to plan. Deciding to set up a tow early can save time and prevent the deterioration of the situation, especially when the casualty regards towing as some kind of defeat, to be put-off as long as possible.

Communication is the key to any towing scenario, confusion can have people pulling in different directions (literally). Towing increases our independence in that we can get each other out of trouble, however... before you start towing ask yourself if you need external assistance and be prepared to call it up. As with any other safety situation look after yourself first then the rest of the group and finally the casualty. It also helps to be well practised – if you are in the unfortunate position of having to tow for a long distance in conditions that are less than ideal then now is not the time to start worrying about your system.

TOP TIPS FOR TOWING:

- Your towing system should be easy to attach.

- It should also be easy to release.

- Choose brightly coloured rope so you can spot it.

- A built-in shock absorber is highly advantageous in anything but flat calm conditions.

- Be able to adjust the length of your system between five and fifteen metres.

- Add a float to the free end of your line.

- Clip onto the deckline from below, to correctly orientate your clip/karabiner and guard against accidental release.

- Carry a knife close to hand just in case the worst should happen and you need to cut free of the system.

fig. 6.40 Commercially available personal towline pouch, with quick release camming buckle on the belt, float and shock absorber (bungee sheathed in tubular tape as failsafe).

WARNING

One thing that you must never do when towing a sea kayak is to use a buoyancy aid with a whitewater chest-harness to tow from. Although this would seem to fit most of the criteria above, the anchor point is too high and there is a chance of serious injury.

fig. 6.41 Clip onto decklines from underneath, leaving the snap gate clear of the boat.

Keep it simple – uncomplicated tows work best. If there are multiple lines and towing paddlers then the chances are that everything will become entangled with everything else and will take more time to sort out than if one person was towing in the first place.

6.11   CONTACT TOWS

Hold – when close to rocks, and speed of attachment is important a contact tow works well. This involves you being able to position yourself within holding range of the casualty. The casualty holds your bow or stern then you can paddle both of you away from danger, keeping the other kayak under your arm.

fig. 6.42 A short line kept across the foredeck to assist with short tows.

Clip in – as above but with the benefit of a short length of line with a clip attached, this is suitable for use over a slightly longer distance.

'V' push – when the casualty requires support but there is not time to arrange a more complex tow. Have an assistant raft together with the casualty and place the bow of your kayak between them. As you paddle you will have to reach over both kayaks to get your blade in the water which may involve sliding your paddle to extend your reach.

6.12   ROPED TOWS

fig. 6.43 (top to bottom) Cam cleat, velcro patches (to secure rope bag) and fairlead.

Boat mounted – there is no easy way of transferring this tow to another person, unless their kayak is already fitted out for towing (strengthened deck, cam cleat and fairlead). However there is much less strain placed on your body than any other system. A quick release must be fitted, within easy reach to ditch the whole system in an instant.

Waist mounted – this can be transferred easily between paddlers (and between boats if you have several) to keep everyone involved. Some folk, especially those with short backs, find it a bit uncomfortable due to the strain taken on your waist. Again a quick release must be fitted.

If the casualty requires extra support whilst being towed, a trailing low brace works well and is preferable to an assistant coming alongside to support them.

LENGTH OF TOW

Into the wind – keep the tow as short as possible but make sure the following kayak has room to swing from side to side. Have the casualty keep their skeg retracted.

With the wind – ideally match the wavelength of the swell, with both kayaks surfing at roughly the same time; in practice though it is a case of 'longer is better'. If the casualty deploys their skeg their kayak should stay in line behind yours.

Across the wind – roughly a boat length gap between kayaks is desirable. Requires most communication with the casualty to make progress, both of you will probably have to use a bit of skeg for control. As the rescuer you have to make the decisions.

6.13 CALLING FOR ASSISTANCE

Sometime you may just have to seek rescue from outside your group. If you are able to contact another water user in the vicinity it is reasonable to expect them to come to your aid. Getting from your kayak and into their boat might well be very difficult and could result in you losing your kayak and all your equipment (make sure your name, postcode and telephone number are displayed inside). This is even more of a problem when being rescued by helicopter, as they will definitely not even make any attempt to recover your kayak.

6.14 VHF RADIO

When you use your VHF radio to summon assistance from any source you should ideally have been trained in its use and have a licence. There is a certain jargon-based communication strategy that allows for clear understanding of the details of the incident.

Mayday – Distress calls. Coming from the French language *m'aidez* (assist me) indicates that a boat or person is threatened by grave and imminent danger and requires immediate assistance. This type of call has absolute priority over all other radio traffic, upon hearing a Mayday call all other communication must stop.

Pan-pan – Urgency call. Used when the person sending the message has a very urgent message to transmit concerning the safety of a boat (or other vehicle) or person. Should be used when safety is at stake but a Mayday signal is not yet justified.

Sécurité – The safety call. These are generally addressed to 'all stations' and although the original call is made on channel 16 the traffic is moved to another suitable channel. Use of Sécurité indicates that the sending station is about to transmit a message containing important navigation or meteorological information.

fig. 6.44 Be ready to use your VHF handset when you need them most. Know your call sign and radio procedures – don't be afraid to use it in non-distress situations to keep your hand in.

6.15 HELICOPTER RESCUE

fig. 6.45 Search & Rescue helicopter. Photo: Nigel Dennis

If a boat comes to your aid, rescue will be reasonably straightforward as communication is not too difficult, the crew will tell you exactly what they want you to do. With a rescue helicopter it is very different. The noise together with the force of the downdraught combines to completely numb your senses. Communication is all but impossible and there is normally a sturdy bloke dangling on the end of a piece of wire, which is loaded with static electricity. A good idea, if you face this situation, is to brief the folk you are with about the noise and the fact that none of you will be able to communicate when the helicopter is overhead. Ensure everything is well tied on and that everyone holds onto each other's kayak as firmly as possible.

As the aircraft approaches from downwind it will most likely make a couple of passes overhead to give the pilot an overview of the rescue area. Then a smoke canister is dropped which allows them to better assess the wind direction and speed. After this the crew will often let down a 'highline'. This is a long piece of strong cord with a weighted bag on the end, this line will be positioned just in the water and then manoeuvred into your hands by the pilot and winchman. Pull in the line as the winchman is lowered from the helicopter, making sure that it does not get tangled up in your equipment. The winchman guides the pilot by using hand signals and he generally drops into the water close to you. It is very important that you do not try to catch him, as the shock from the static can be quite substantial. The highline is generally released from the winch wire and left with the remaining group or jettisoned completely.

The easiest rescue from the crew's point of view is a swimmer in the water, but sometimes this is not possible due to injuries the casualty may have. It is possible for them to lift from a raft of kayaks but you can bet your best piece of kit that things will get broken, as the winchman will be wearing a survival suit equipped with anti-slip boots.

The pilot and crew of Search and Rescue helicopters are a very well trained and highly skilled group of people. If you are at all unsure of what you should do – do nothing. They will adapt their rescue to suit the developing situation. Having a helicopter hover above you when you are fit and well is one thing, being involved in a rescue with one must be quite another.

If you use your VHF radio to communicate it will most likely be on channel 16, the crew however will communicate with other rescuers on channel 0 which is available only to rescue agencies.

"A couple of guys I met a long time ago were paddling off the East Coast of Scotland near Arbroath. One capsized then wet exited, the other was unable to manoeuvre close enough to perform a rescue. There was a strong offshore wind blowing and both ended up in the water, fortunately someone walking their dog along the cliff top path saw them and raised the alarm. The lifeboat and helicopter were sent to assist and the guys ended up being in the water for around ninety minutes before being lifted into the chopper, their kayaks and other equipment being left as offerings to the ocean. After a night in hospital they returned home and started looking for their boats, one they found a few miles from where the incident took place and it was undamaged. A couple of months later they received a telephone call from a Norwegian fisherman who had found a kayak with a telephone number inside. They made arrangements to collect the boat and supply the fisherman with some malt whisky."

6.16   THANK YOUR RESCUER

In a rescue situation, things go wrong, things get lost. If everything comes out alright in the wash, there is reason to be grateful.

Keep account of your kit, especially in high winds or strong currents. In a tidal race, because everything is drifting with the current, there is a good chance of losing some part of equipment if it is not properly secured to body or boat. I once lost my carbon paddle when assessing an award where the candidates had to perform rescues of varying magnitude. I was the unconscious victim and let go! After putting an advert in the local paper it was found by a local about two months later.

In all rescue situations, if it is you who has been in the water, remember to thank your rescuer. Find out what their favourite tipple is and supply them with a bottle. This will ensure that the next time they have to rescue you, they will be right there. It will also set up the loop so that if they have to call on your services, you will find yourself the recipient of something you enjoy!

6.17   FIRST AID AT SEA

Performing first aid whilst afloat is a necessary skill and the best preparation is practice. Simple things become more difficult and even a sticking plaster becomes a major challenge. The best option is to have a small first aid kit handy and include in it the things that you are most likely to need based on your experience. Here are a few incidents I have had to deal with and the equipment I carry to enable me to deal with them satisfactorily.

+ BLISTERS – caused anywhere there is rubbing but generally on the hands. The problem here is that the skin is wet and there is no way to dry it and then keep it dry so any dressing you attach will have to be long enough to be stuck onto itself. Duct tape, although very good, does not stretch and care must be taken that it is not applied too tightly, cutting off the circulation. Brown parcel tape is pretty effective and provides a slippery surface for the paddle to slide over. Electrical insulating tape is also good as it has a bit of give and provides a bit more protection due to its thickness. If the blister has de-roofed then a clean dry dressing applied ashore is the best bet.

+ CUTS on hands from knife, shell, rock or whatever – these are most likely going to have dirt in them and therefore good wound management is vital. Unless you are paddling in very polluted waters, the sea is a very good medium for initial cleaning of the cut. If the bleeding is profuse, elevate and apply pressure as in any first aid situation. Apply a dressing and then waterproof tape stuck onto itself to secure. If the cut is on the palm of the hand then you will most likely have to tow the casualty, possibly with support, until a landing can be made and things dealt with with more care.

fig. 6.46
Portuguese
man-of-war.
Photo: NOAA

+ JELLYFISH STINGS – best treatment is avoidance. If stung do not rub as this causes the poison sac to 'fire' again. Stings stay attached to your skin with minute barbs and the best way to remove these is by using a plastic card to 'shave' the affected area with a gloved hand, then rinse. An ice pack will ease the pain and slow the progress of the poison. In extreme cases you may have to administer antihistamine, either topically as a spray or crushed, under the tongue. There is a risk of anaphylactic shock.

Portuguese man-of-war *(Physalia physalis)* is not a jellyfish but a colony of polyps. Recognised by its oval shaped transparent float with crest, its tentacles may be tens of metres long. They are generally found in warm tropical and subtropical zones such as the Gulf Stream waters but occasionally they may be blown on the wind into British waters.

Urine is often said to be an effective remedy for jellyfish stings. This is not unfounded but for all severe stings, applying vinegar or urine, or washing the area before the poison sacks have been removed will cause a rapid release of poison into the victim.

✛ **TENOSYNOVITIS** – again the best treatment is complete avoidance. The onset of this painful complaint is gradual and therefore is not generally an on-the-water problem. If it does happen then 'rest is best' but this will severely curtail your trip. Strapping the affected wrist to stop movement in any plane is beneficial although swelling will possibly occur and any brace or strapping will require to be loosened. A specially designed brace is available but this is too large to be carried on your person and is best dealt with ashore.

✛ **SEASICKNESS** – completely debilitating if you are a sufferer. Best remedy is to take preventative medication. The downside to most of these is that there is a risk of drowsiness, not the best thing whilst you are in a kayak! Unfortunately if you are on the water and start to feel the effects of motion sickness there is little you can do. Support and tow is the best bet but ensure the supporter has a strong stomach. I suffer from motion sickness when I am travelling on big boats and have found a drug called 'Buccastem' helps me. This is placed between lip and gum and allowed to dissolve. The benefit over the others I have tried is that you can administer this even after you have started to feel sick and the tablet remains in place when you are throwing up. Most folks have very little energy left after suffering from seasickness so be aware that you might well have to tow for a considerable time.

✛ **HYPOGLYCAEMIA** – normally caused by not eating enough, often enough. Also associated with diabetes. The effects of this can be confused with mild hypothermia with most sufferers becoming lethargic and moody. The quick-fix is to make them eat something which has a mixture of carbohydrates, both simple and complex and then ensure they are eating enough throughout the rest of the trip. For a longer-term solution check that folks have had enough breakfast and are taking on enough calories during the day. High-energy bars and sachets are easily available, so everyone can carry something for such an occurrence.

✛ **DEHYDRATION** – generally the first signs are a feeling of being thirsty followed by headaches. Caused by lack of fluid intake either because the paddler doesn't want to have to remove loads of clothing to relieve themselves or through illness (seasickness or diarrhoea). Ensure you drink plenty whilst you are on the water and ashore, a minimum of four litres a day when the weather is warm or when you are exerting yourself. There are many types of drinking bladder available with some even having fittings to allow fixing to a buoyancy aid.

✛ **SUN RELATED INJURIES** – sunburn and blisters, treat as you would any other burn by immersing in cold water then covering with a light dressing. Prevention is always the best cure so remember 'slip-slap-slop'. Slip into a long sleeved protective shirt, Slap on a wide brimmed hat and Slop on plenty of high factor sunscreen. Reflected light also gives an eye injury similar to snow blindness, treatment is rest and shade but prevention is easier. Wear sunglasses and ensure they block 100% UVA and UVB.

✚ **CPR/EAV** (Cardiopulmonary Rescusitation / Expired Air Ventilation) – whilst afloat are not the easiest things to do but are possible with a bit of thought.

For **EAV**, if the casualty is in the water, the best bet is to get into the water beside them. Holding the end grab on your kayak with your right hand, bring their head over this arm until their neck is positioned on top of your arm. Use your left hand to hold them here, at the same time pinching their nose between thumb and index finger, perform your rescue breaths as instructed during your first aid training. If the casualty is not in the water then lying them across the deck of a group of rafted kayaks makes a suitable platform but it is not the easiest thing to do especially as whoever is doing the breathing for the casualty will probably have to get out of their kayak too.

CPR can only be carried out on a flat hard surface. The only option here is to make a raft, lift the casualty onto this, then perform **CPR** in the normal manner at the same time ensuring there is a kayak below the part of their chest you are compressing.

Most First Aid courses assume 'expert medical help' will arrive within thirty minutes. If you are in the situation of having to perform **CPR/EAV** on any person in a wilderness environment, then there are a few basic rules.

◎ The first thing you must do is put out a **Mayday** call on your VHF radio.

◎ Assess the situation and the whole group.

◎ Think very carefully before you get into the water beside any casualty.

◎ Do what you can, but do not overstretch your capabilities.

◎ Be prepared to make a decision that you will have
  to live with for the rest of your life.

✚ **HYPOTHERMIA** – dealing with this when afloat is not too easy. As when ashore the casualty has to be isolated from the environment, re-warmed, morale maintained, food and drink intake monitored, made as comfortable as possible and monitored for improvement or decline. By towing the afflicted person backwards with support immediately removes them from the environment, put a hat on to minimise heat loss upwards. If you have a 'storm cag' put this on, attach the waist around the cockpit then add all of the other insulating materials. Wrap in a bivvi bag or group shelter and give warm drink and high-energy foods. Ensure the support person is able to look after themselves as well as the victim and that everything is available to them as it is required.

✚ **HYPERTHERMIA** – this is not quite as common, especially in our northern waters, but does happen. Ensure the casualty has plenty of fluid intake and shade from the sun. Immerse in the water gradually by splashing first then a more continued soaking. Keep wet clothes on as the heat energy from the casualty is absorbed by their clothing to evaporate the water. Placing the wrists and ankles in the water helps as the blood flow is very close to the surface in these areas. One thing to be mindful of is the risk of overcooling and then having to deal with a hypothermic victim.

✚ **RECOVERY OF AN UNCONSCIOUS SWIMMER** – if there is a group of you it is possible to raft the kayaks together and then standing on the deck lift the casualty from the water. Another method is to use the 'scoop' rescue mentioned earlier.

✚ **LIGHTNING STRIKE** – you don't want to have to deal with this. If thunder and lightning are forecast get off the water and behave like a mountaineer. Lightning is attracted by tall objects, jumps gaps and travels along wet surfaces. So avoid sheltering in caves or under overhangs, sit down in the open on a well drained surface such as pebbles or sand, and if possible insulate yourself from the ground.

"Once when paddling in the Firth of Clyde we were crossing Brodick Bay on Arran when there was an unexpected thunderstorm nearby. We were around two miles from land and I was at the back of the group. Being concerned I was looking around not quite knowing what to expect when I noticed that everyone in front was glowing. I had never seen Saint Elmo's Fire before and fortunately have not since."

✚ **DISLOCATED SHOULDER** – there is very little you can do whilst afloat except reassure the patient and support the arm in the most comfortable position. They will let you know where that is! As with most other injury scenarios a supported tow is the way to go.

VERY IMPORTANT

Every time you deal with any incident on the sea assume that everyone in the group is suffering from 'the Three Hippos'

◎ **Hypothermia**

◎ **Hypoglycaemia**

◎ **'Hypo'-hydration**

Treat accordingly and remember that you are part of the group too!

PLATE X *Duncan Winning journeys to Igdlorssuit to visit the family
of the kayak builder Emanuele Kornielsen in 2004.*

PLATE XI *Exploring Ummannaq Fiord, North West Greenland.*

7 Seamanship

Seamanship is the art of living according to the ways and rules of the sea. It requires, along with knowledge, a healthy respect for the sea and an aptitude for anticipation. You must accept absolutely, responsibility for your actions. You cannot learn seamanship entirely from books alone, nor even from other people, but it is possible to get a good head start this way. The lessons are only driven home when you spend time on the water making mistakes and learning from them.

"The ocean often gives us the test before thinking to give the lesson" – *Anon*

The preceding chapters have perhaps dealt with your preparation for going to sea, and what follows are chapters which give pointers of how to deal with it once you are amongst it. In this chapter I'll introduce a few seemingly disparate key ideas and then the following chapters will deal in more depth with the key aspects of seamanship (Navigation, Weather, Reading the Water, and so on).

7.1 THE UNITS OF THE SEA

As well as sound of body, we must also be sound of mind, this applies most practically to arithmetic – calculating speed, distance and time is important for sea kayakers. Because you do not have easy access to a calculator, it is best if you are able to perform the sums you need most often in your head. This only comes through practice for most of us.

It is a good habit to use nautical miles for your calculations as well as your speed; all of the information you will find on charts and in marine publications will be in this format. As most people are used to dealing with topographic maps, it makes sense to use a familiar unit of measurement such as kilometres, but one nautical mile is as near 2km as makes little difference to most calculations you will make.

1 metre = 3.281 feet
1 statute mile = 1.609 kilometres
1 nautical mile = 1.15077945 statute miles

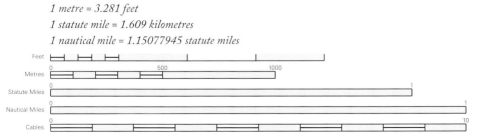

DIRECTIONS:

Wind direction – is stated as where wind is blowing from. A southerly wind is from the south, blowing to the north.

Tide direction – is stated as where the tide is flowing towards. So a south-going tide flows south.

fig. 7.1 Buoy behaviour – a navigation buoy will tilt downstream, a small lobster pot buoy may be completely submerged, creating a wave.

7.2 WEATHER FORECASTING

Remember that a weather forecast is exactly that - a prediction. We must interpret the information forecasters give and apply our knowledge of an area and its associated landforms to perhaps come up with a completely different outlook. Now refer to Chapter 10, Weather.

7.3 JUDGING TIME & DISTANCE

RESOLVABLE DETAIL METHOD (distance):

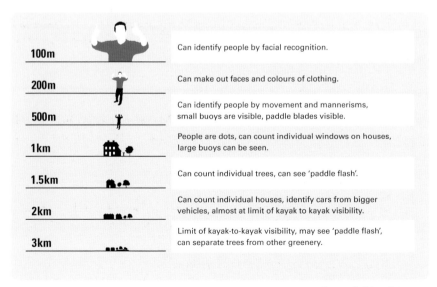

Distance	Detail
100m	Can identify people by facial recognition.
200m	Can make out faces and colours of clothing.
500m	Can identify people by movement and mannerisms, small buoys are visible, paddle blades visible.
1km	People are dots, can count individual windows on houses, large buoys can be seen.
1.5km	Can count individual trees, can see 'paddle flash'.
2km	Can count individual houses, identify cars from bigger vehicles, almost at limit of kayak to kayak visibility.
3km	Limit of kayak-to-kayak visibility, may see 'paddle flash', can separate trees from other greenery.

fig. 7.2 Judging distance.

FINGER SEXTANT METHOD (time):

The sun appears to move across the sky and takes twenty-four hours to move 360°. Using mental arithmetic, we find that in one hour it moves 15° and in four minutes approximately 1°. The width of an average finger held at arm's length is approximately 2°. This means that if we look at the sun when it is setting and it is four finger widths above the horizon, there are approximately thirty minutes until sunset.

7.4 COLLISION COURSE

If you are paddling on a bearing and another water user is heading on a converging course, how can you tell whether you will pass in front, collide or pass behind?

Transit – Look at the front of the approaching vessel and make a transit on the bow and a point in the distance. If the gap increases you will pass in front of it, if the gap stays constant you will collide and if the gap decreases you will pass behind. This assumes that both your and their courses remain constant.

Angle – Another similar method is to look at the relative angle between the front of your kayak and their bow. If the angle remains the same you will collide, if it increases you will pass in front and if it decreases you will pass behind.

If you are at all unsure whether you are on a collision course or not, make a definite change of direction. If you are head on or they are coming up from behind you (remember that there is a good chance they haven't seen you in either case) a 90° change of course is best. Either way, make it prompt and obvious!

7.5 LOOKING AFTER THE ENVIRONMENT

As probably the most ecological method of transport afloat, it is a good idea to know a bit about your environment. Here are some thoughts on the things that are important to me:

◎ The wildlife in all its forms. Be aware of breeding
   seasons, habitats and vulnerable species.

◎ Plastic containers, rope etc. take an absolute age to degrade, try to pick
   up at least three pieces of litter every time you are on the water.

◎ Learn a bit about the different types of seaweed you are tramping
   through, some are pretty rare and most can be eaten.

◎ Messing about with other people's crab and lobster pots is a bad idea. The folk that put these pots out are generally either trying to make a living or feed their families. If you steal from them you are a thief. Talking to the fishermen may get you some of their catch.

◎ Eat mussels if you can. Pick them from vertical rock faces around low water. You will mostly find these bivalves close to where there is a fresh water stream coming into the sea. Discard any which are open before cooking and any which do not open after cooking. The reason we are told not to eat shellfish when there is not an 'R' in the month is to do with the quality of the meat as they will have spawned (muscle flesh is mostly gonad) and not the effect of the tidal bloom or algae.

◎ If you fish… fish! (I can never seem to manage to catch fewer than six mackerel when I try, if I have less lures on my line I catch nothing.) There is nothing you can catch which you cannot eat.

◎ If you have to have a fire, make it a small one and tidy up afterwards. If possible light it below the high water mark and be sure you don't put any plastic items onto it. You would not believe the number of times I have found fire remains with a conglomerate of melted fish box. Where you find wood that looks as if it has been stacked to dry, it probably has. Leave this alone and collect some for yourself.

◎ Do not ever feed the animals you meet, they will become pests and will bother the next group that comes in your wake. Just think of the seagulls at your local put-in…

◎ Going to the loo below the high water mark is a sensible idea, cover your waste with some stones and burn the paper. If this is not possible, carry a small trowel and bury well away from any watercourse or path, again burn your paper.

◎ Carry out all your rubbish and other people's too. Put it in the first bin you come across.

fig. 7.3
Observing the behaviour of icebergs, North West Greenland.

7.6 LOOKING AFTER YOURSELF

When you are on the water you have to take care of your exposed parts. The reflection of the sun on the water, with the wind, combine to give extreme exposure.

Hats – Wear a big brimmed hat to protect your face, ears and back of your neck. A baseball cap will shade your face only.

Sunglasses – are a must as, even on overcast days, the glare coming off the water is substantial. Choose good quality ones which block 100% UVA and UVB. Some companies manufacture these protective glasses with clear, or almost clear, lenses. In all cases it is a good idea to have your shades secured with a retainer.

Sunscreen – When you apply sunscreen, use the backs of your hands (better still, get someone else to apply it for you). This ensures you have the exposed areas covered and also that you can still grip your paddle. It can be a good idea to carry surfboard wax to rub onto your paddle shaft after you have put your sunscreen on, as it will give you a bit more grip.

Fluid intake – is very important for performance and keeping headaches at bay; remember that if you begin to feel thirsty you are already around one litre dehydrated! Use anything that you can access easily whilst paddling. Ideally this would be some type of bladder system with a flexible tube leading to a bite valve located near your mouth, although any container can be used.

Snacks – for some people are a must and others seem to manage just fine without these energy boosts. It is always a good idea to have some high-energy food easily available throughout the duration of your trip.

7.7 LIMIT OF ADEQUATE RESERVE

This simple rule says that you should always have enough fuel left in the tank to get you to where you want to go. A good way to think about it is to plan a hypothetical paddle to a distant island. For example St Kilda is the destination, leaving from North Uist, a distance of around forty nautical miles and your paddling speed is three knots. Around thirteen hours for the crossing is the likely time you will come up with. Now imagine arriving, or getting to within landing distance and finding that due to sea conditions you are unable to land. Could you turn round and head back to your starting point? For most of us mortals the answer would be no.

On the opposite page is a table, which is a starting point for most paddlers given average fitness and experience. The right-hand column is the 'limit of adequate reserve' and refers to you having paddled eight hours in good conditions, then asks how much longer you could paddle for if necessary if the wind strength changed. All this assumes a base paddling speed of three knots.

Remember that the Beaufort Scale was originally devised for much larger boats than ours; as such it is only a rough guide of what to expect on open water. The wind speeds shown are averages and gusts up to the next force should be anticipated. The sea conditions when close to land will tend to become more severe and funnelling of the wind may happen. This is common along stretches of coast where there are high cliffs.

The probable wave height is based on observations on open water. What you see is based on looking into the wind. How it feels is based on personal experience, it may need modifying for your own use. Your speed with and against the wind direction will vary as your fitness varies. Your limit of adequate reserve will also vary as everyone is different but at least this is a starting point.

Winds – be aware of any weather anomalies that cause interference in the normal pattern of wind speed and direction. During spells of warmer weather a sea breeze is very likely due to the land heating and taking the cooler air from the water to feed the rising thermals. This is not much of a problem for us as kayakers but when the land starts to cool, usually around sunset, we can get some land breezes. Again this is not too big a problem unless there is a physical feature, which accelerates the wind and funnels it at an increased velocity in your direction. This phenomenon normally happens where there is a valley leading from higher ground all the way to the sea. Sometimes the area of wind can be a few hundred metres wide and if the valley is a large one then it could be a few miles wide.

The sea looks rougher if you look into the wind than it does if you are looking at the back of the waves. This is because when you look into the wind you are seeing the full size of the wave as well as the white stuff that is falling down the face towards you.

**You should always have enough fuel left in the tank
to get you to where you want to go.**

fig. 7.4 (opposite) Beaufort Scale & limit of adequate reserve. See fig. 10.5 for photo illustrations of Force 1 to 8.

Beaufort Scale (Bf)	Wind Speed (kt)	Ocean Wave Height* (m)	Seaman's Term	Sea Conditions	Land Conditions	Paddling Conditions	Speed With (kt)	Speed Against (kt)	Limit of Adequate Reserve
Force 0	0	0	Calm	Mirror like.	Smoke rises vertically.	Easy paddling	3	3	Indefinite
Force 1	1 – 3	0	Light air	Almost mirror like.	Smoke drifts with the wind, weather vanes do not move.	Easy paddling.	3	3	Indefinite until sleep takes over
Force 2	4 – 6	0.1	Light breeze	Small wavelets. Crests of glassy appearance, not breaking.	Wind felt on face. Leaves rustle.	Easy paddling.	3	3	8hrs
Force 3	7 – 10	0.4	Gentle breeze	Large wavelets. Crests begin to break; a few white horses.	Leaves and smaller twigs in constant motion. Light flags extended.	Relatively easy paddling Noticeable work paddling into headwind. Novices start to struggle in cross-wind.	3.5	2.75	6hrs
Force 4	11 – 16	1	Moderate breeze	Small waves, frequent white horses.	Dust, leaves and loose paper raised, Small branches begin to move.	Sustained effort into headwind. Following wind starts to become following sea.	3.5	2.75	4hrs
Force 5	17 – 21	2	Fresh breeze	Moderate longer waves. Some foam and spray.	Small trees begin to sway.	Hard effort. Expect paddle flutter – begin to use low paddling style. Cross-winds become difficult.	3.75	2.5	2hrs
Force 6	22 – 27	3	Strong breeze	Large waves with foam crests and some spray.	Large branches move. Whistling heard from overhead wires. Umbrella use becomes difficult.	Very hard effort. Paddle flutter requires control. Limit of practical paddling any distance into headwind. Following sea requires concentration.	4	2.25	1 – 2 hrs
Force 7	28 – 33	4	Moderate gale	Sea heaps up and foam begins to streak.	Whole trees in motion. Resistance felt when walking into the wind.	Strenuous Following seas exhilarating for experienced paddler, but risk of capsize for inexperienced. Paddling across wind very difficult.	4.5	1.5	40 mins – 1.5 hrs
Force 8	34 – 40	5.5	Fresh gale	Moderately high waves with breaking crests forming spindrift. Streaks of foam.	Twigs broken from trees. Cars veer on road.	Very strenuous Lots of concentration required downwind Into the wind for only short distances (less than 0.5km).	4.5	1	20 mins – 1hour
Force 9	41 – 47	7	Strong gale	High waves with dense foam. Wave crests start to roll over. Considerable spray.	Light structure damage, slates blown from roofs.				
Force 10	48 – 55	9	Storm	Very high waves. The sea surface is white and there is considerable tumbling. Visibility reduced.	Trees uprooted. Considerable structural damage.				
Force 11	56 – 63	11.5	Violent storm	Exceptionally high waves.	Widespread structural damage.				
Force 12	> 63	14+	Hurricane	Huge waves. Air filled with foam and spray. Sea completely white with driving spray. Visibility very greatly reduced.	Massive and widespread damage to structures.				

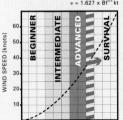

SURVIVAL PADDLING
SEEK SHELTER ON LAND IMMEDIATELY

$v = 1.627 \times Bf^{3/2}$ kt

*average wave height is pertinent to unsheltered west facing Atlantic coastlines such as Argyll, Cornwall & Connaught.

PLATE XII *Navigating in an ice-field brings its own particular problems.*

8 Navigation

Let's begin with a refresher on navigational jargon, and then onto some useful methods.

NAVIGATIONAL JARGON

bearing – the direction of one object from another, eg. the angle from north of some feature from your position.

cable – one tenth of a nautical mile (apprx. 200m).

course – the direction you are intending to steer.

cocked hat – bearings from three points forming triangular intersection, giving your position in the vicinity of the triangle (mountaineers call this a resection). The size of the triangle is a rough indicator of the reliability of your **position fix**.

current – flow of water in a particular direction. Especially ocean currents generated by the wind or thermohaline circulation, which have little effect inshore. Often used when actually referring to tidal streams.

heading – the direction your kayak is pointing. **nb.** rarely identical to your **course**.

knot – unit of speed equivalent to one nautical mile per hour (1 knot = 1 nautical mile per hour).

latitude – the angle between the earth's centre and your position north or south of the equator. The equator is 0°, north or south poles are 90°. Lines of similar latitude are called parallels of latitude.

longitude – the angle between the Prime Meridian 0° (a line which segments the earth from pole to pole, intersecting Greenwich, UK) and your position east or west. Lines of similar longitude are meridians of longitude.

magnetic deviation – the error induced in a compass by nearby magnetic fields, not normally a problem on a kayak as ferrous metals and electrical goods can be stowed well away from the compass.

magnetic declination – see **magnetic variation**.

magnetic north – the earth's north magnetic pole and the point toward which your compass points.

magnetic variation – the angle between the local magnetic field (the direction the compass points) and true north. The variation is positive when the magnetic north is east of true north. Variation changes from place to place and year to year and is noted on the compass rose on a chart. Printed on the magnetic north arrow the information also includes the rate of annual change.

nautical mile – a unit of distance equivalent to one minute of latitude, 1852 metres. One degree of latitude = 60′ = 60 nautical miles. Also a geographical mile.

neap tides – occur around the first and third phases of the moon (half moon) when the moon's gravitational pull on the oceans is at right angles to that of the sun. This reduces the tidal range, producing lower highs and higher lows. Also neaps. See **spring tides**.

position fix – a measured determination of where you are. Given as latitude then longitude and expressed as degrees and minutes with seconds or a decimal part of a minute to pinpoint position. For example, St Kilda 57°50′N 8°30′W.

spring tides – occur around the new moon and full moon when the moon's gravitational pull on the oceans is in line with that of the sun. This increases the tidal range, producing higher highs and lower lows. Also springs. See **neap tides**.

tidal stream – flow of water in a particular direction of tidal movement.

tide – the vertical displacement of water by the gravitational pull of the sun and moon.

true north – the direction of the north pole.

This is covered in many other manuals; what we will look at here is the seat-of-the-pants type of navigating commonly known as dead reckoning. Navigation is a science. In a kayak however it is also an art. Other water users have speedometers fitted to their craft in order to tell their speed; we must rely on feel and our knowledge of that feeling. We could, of course, use GPS but I think that takes a lot of the fun out of the sport and turns the art back into science.

> ### "If you have to work out where you are, you're halfway to being lost."
> ### Donald Thomson

8.1 TOOLS OF THE TRADE

Navigating a sea kayak is more problematic than a larger boat; you cannot spread your chart or map out on a table to work at the problem. Everything has to be carried out on a sloping deck less than an arm's length wide, normally with a peak in the middle. Out go the normal tools of the marine-based navigator, parallel rules and dividers. In come the more basic tools of the sea kayaker: watch, orienteering-type compass, fingers and eyes.

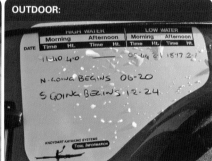

fig. 8.1 Chart, dividers and parallel rules. In the chart room there's plenty of room for precision instuments.

fig. 8.2 Every centimetre of deck space is valuable, a white fablon 'deck slate' can help you make notes with a chinograph pencil right next to the cockpit.

8.2   AWARENESS

Knowing where you are all the time is a skill that cannot be overstated. Bear in mind that a good navigator is constantly aware of the surroundings. Most navigation can be done without the compass in good weather; an experienced navigator absorbs details of the situation and compares this with the chart (keeping the two matched).

Knowing which approximate direction you are travelling without having to look at your compass is a skill that requires thought until it becomes second nature. In the northern hemisphere the sun travels towards the south at midday, in the southern hemisphere it tracks in a northerly direction.

When paddling in the southern hemisphere it took me three weeks to become used to this different position of the sun. I had to consciously observe and rethink our direction. After returning home I had to readjust my internal compass.

Assuming that you know your starting point, your direction of travel, speed and elapsed time of journey, you should be able to estimate your position reasonably accurately. When paddling along a coastline, you should know what speed you are paddling at and what the tidal influence is, if there is any. From this you can mentally tick off the various landmarks as you pass them. When paddling at three knots, you cover one tenth of a nautical mile every two minutes.

By carefully observing the coastline and your chart you should be able to see streams as they pass, small promontories, bays and charted rocks. These points are all confirming your position along the coast (nb. you cannot tell from this method how far offshore you are).

8.3   DOUBLING THE BOW ANGLE

A simple method for finding your distance from a fixed point is by 'doubling your bow angle'. Spot a conspicuous landmark and take an approximate angle on it in relation to your course, time how long it takes for you to double that angle. Discounting the effects of wind or tide – this time is the same as the time you are from the landmark. 45° and 90° are the easiest angles to visualise, but in effect for any given pair of angles they form two vertices of an isoscelese triangle. For further explanation see the diagram overleaf.

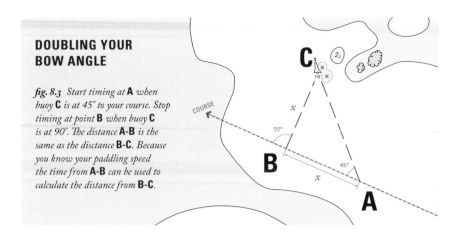

DOUBLING YOUR BOW ANGLE

*fig. 8.3 Start timing at **A** when buoy **C** is at 45° to your course. Stop timing at point **B** when buoy **C** is at 90°. The distance **A-B** is the same as the distance **B-C**. Because you know your paddling speed the time from **A-B** can be used to calculate the distance from **B-C**.*

From this you should be able to determine the next safe landing spot or how close you are to the problem area you recognised during your tabletop planning at home. Also, by using this type of navigation you can keep constant check on your position, very valuable should anything untoward happen.

8.4 FIXING POSITION

By using a combination of techniques it is possible to get a reasonably accurate fix on your position. With three or more points of reference it is possible to triangulate a 'cocked hat' or find the intersection of two transits.

Cocked hat – taking three bearings on identifiable objects and noting these on your chart then plotting the lines will give you the most accurate fix within the percentage error caused by the movement of a sea kayak. This works best if the three points are equally spread through the 360° of the compass, but will still give reasonable accuracy if two are closer together. Your position, when plotted, will be somewhere close to or inside the triangle or 'cocked hat' that is produced when drawing the lines.

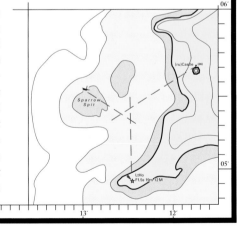

fig. 8.4 Finding a cocked hat.

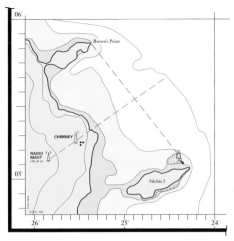

Transit intersect – paddling along a transit between two identifiable points gives you a line upon which you are travelling. If you now find a landmark off to the side and take a bearing on it, then transfer this to your chart, that will be your position. Or if you can draw another transit from two landmarks (as shown in the diagram) you can fix your position with some accuracy without a compass.

fig. 8.5 Intersection of two transits.

8.5 MAGNETIC VARIATION

Remember that north on your chart is not the same as north on your compass (see page 93).

Error West compass Best
—
Error East compass Least

That is to say, in order to convert true north on your chart to the magnetic north on your compass – add the value if it is quoted as 'west' magnetic **variation** – subtract the value if it is quoted as 'east' magnetic **variation**. For example if the course taken from your chart is 090° T (True) and **variation** is 8° W (West), the direction you need to paddle in using the compass is 098° M (Magnetic). If the **variation** is 8° E (East) the direction according to the compass would be 082° M.

The rhyme still works when you take a bearing with your compass and need to convert it to use it on the chart. Just make sure that if **variation** is west your compass has a bigger number than your chart ('compass best') and if it is east it is a smaller number than your chart ('compass least'). For example you point your boat at an object and the **compass** reads 150° M and **variation** is 5° W. The direction to plot on the **chart** would be 145° T.

It does not matter whether you do your working out with true or magnetic bearings as long as you are constant; just remember to convert to what is required.

8.6 AIMING OFF

Aiming off is a method of navigation that ensures you know where you are on a given stretch of coast. Imagine you are heading towards an island and there is only one landing spot. If you took a bearing on this place and then paddled towards it as accurately as you are able, when you reached the land you would not know whether to turn left or right to get to your chosen spot. If you were to aim off to one side you would then know which way to turn. It is always best to aim off upwind or up tide, this way you will drift towards your destination.

8.7 PADDLING SPEED

There are a few satisfactory ways to find out your normal paddling speed.

Measure a distance on a chart using recognisable features and then paddle this distance, making note of your travel time. Use the formula:

$$paddling\ speed\ (kn) = \frac{distance\ (Nm)}{time\ (mins)} \times 60$$

How far do you travel per stroke? Assuming that you now know what your paddling speed is when there are no other influences, it is a relatively easy job to work out how many paddle strokes you take to cover a given distance. Suppose for the moment that your paddling speed is three knots. In twenty minutes you will have covered one nautical mile, and in two minutes, a tenth of a nautical mile.

By the same means, if you paddle for two minutes and count your paddle strokes on one side only you will come up with a number for yourself, given your kayak and paddle. Having a calculation of distance paddled in this way allows you to be accurate in your navigating to within something like 10m. Most people, irrespective of size, weight or strength, find that the number of strokes on one side is between 25 and 30 per minute.

Or you could have someone alongside in a powered boat with a speedometer. Likewise you could use a GPS receiver to record your speed and position automatically.

PLATE XIII *Kayaks 180 metres below Barra Head,*
Outer Hebrides.

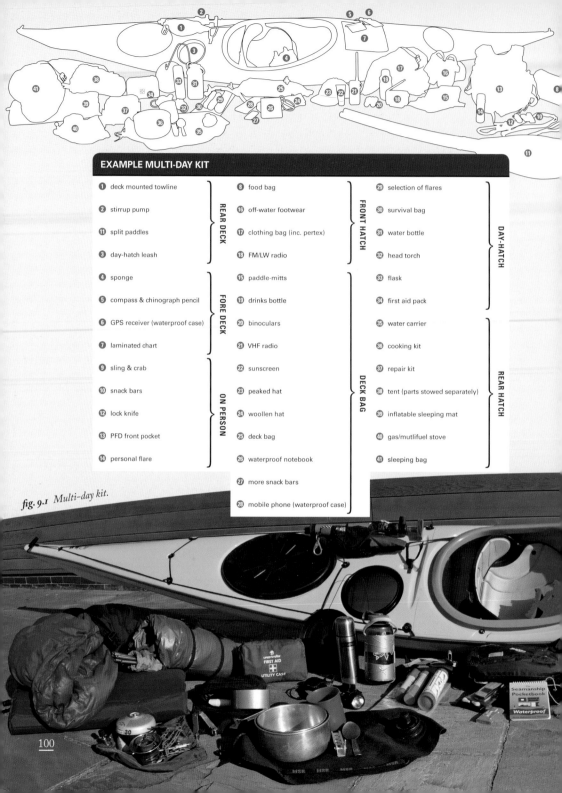

EXAMPLE MULTI-DAY KIT

REAR DECK
1. deck mounted towline
2. stirrup pump
11. split paddles
3. day-hatch leash

FORE DECK
4. sponge
5. compass & chinograph pencil
6. GPS receiver (waterproof case)
7. laminated chart

ON PERSON
9. sling & crab
10. snack bars
12. lock knife
13. PFD front pocket
14. personal flare

FRONT HATCH
8. food bag
16. off-water footwear
17. clothing bag (inc. pertex)
18. FM/LW radio

DECK BAG
15. paddle-mitts
19. drinks bottle
20. binoculars
21. VHF radio
22. sunscreen
23. peaked hat
24. woollen hat
25. deck bag
26. waterproof notebook
27. more snack bars
28. mobile phone (waterproof case)

DAY-HATCH
29. selection of flares
30. survival bag
31. water bottle
32. head torch
33. flask
34. first aid pack

REAR HATCH
35. water carrier
36. cooking kit
37. repair kit
38. tent (parts stowed separately)
39. inflatable sleeping mat
40. gas/mutlifuel stove
41. sleeping bag

fig. 9.1 Multi-day kit.

9 Equipment

By far the most important advice I can give about equipment is to keep it clean, tidy and in a serviceable condition. Look after your kit and it will look after you. What's more, by paying attention to the details, everything you use on the sea will last a good bit longer.

AFTER EVERY USE (where practical)

◎ Wash everything in fresh water. When salt water dries it leaves a very abrasive residue, this will destroy any softwear quicker than you could by dragging it across a beach.

◎ Wash the salt from your paddle, especially if it is the Paddlok type and check for damage, repairing any nicks with a suitable sticky substance - two-part epoxy glue works well.

◎ Dry everything completely before storing for any length of time.

◎ Buoyancy aids were not designed as seats, don't use them for this unless for insulation in an emergency.

◎ Follow the manufacturer's care instructions to get best life from your garment.

"Look after your equipment and it will look after you"

MONTHLY MAINTENANCE (if you paddle regularly)

Wash out your kayak to get rid of any salt or sand, pay particular attention to the footrests if they are of the adjustable type. Apply an oil-free lubricant, such as those used by cyclists, to any moving parts. If you use a lubricant which has oil as a base then sand will stick to everything and the whole assembly will seize up and will require replacement sooner than you might think. Check skeg control for free movement and replace cable if required. Check rudder cables and lifting mechanism for wear and damage; repair and replace as necessary. Most of these cables have a useful lifespan of two to four years, depending on abuse, and should see you through that length of time without any problems.

BIANNUAL MAINTENANCE

Wash the hatch covers whatever type they are, allow them to dry and then treat with a silicone-based protector, this is more important for the flexible rubber type found on most kayaks now. Storing in a dark area while not in use will prolong their useful life. Any kit (repair and first aid) that remains in a waterproof container for a long period should be checked and dried out at least a couple of times a year. It wouldn't be the first time that I have gone into a waterproof bag and found some items unusable.

9.1 FIRST AID KIT

I keep my first aid kit in a fold-out wash bag which is waterproofed by placing inside a roll down dry bag. This allows me to open the bag then lay things out as I need them. At a glance I can see if there is anything that requires replacing. Total weight is around 500 grams.

◎ **Surgical gloves & face mask** (kept at top of container).

◎ **Antacid**

◎ **Antihistamine** (tablets and spray*) – very useful for jellyfish stings where relief is generally required pretty quickly.

◎ **Antiseptic cream** or lotion (try to get one which contains iodine, as this kills most bugs you can get from a cut from a shell).

◎ **Cotton bandage** (or open wove bandage).

◎ **Crepe bandage** – great for sprains and strains especially of the forearm, could also use tubular bandage.

◎ **Forceps or tweezers**

* Useful items to carry in a waterproof container on your person, in addition to those within the main kit.

◎ **Gauze swabs**

◎ **Moleskin or Second Skin** (for padding badly blistered areas).

◎ **Non-adherent dressings**, e.g Melolin.

◎ **Safety Pins*** (securing sleeve onto jacket in a shoulder dislocation).

◎ **Scissors** (Tuff Cut type are pretty useful and generally do not corrode).

◎ **Sterile scalpel**

◎ **Steri-strips*** or butterfly sutures.

◎ **Sticking plasters** – assorted sizes (duct tape* can be used but has no stretch).

◎ **Sunscreen**

◎ **Triangular bandages x 2** (used for general bandaging as well as immobilisation of injured limbs).

◎ **Zinc oxide tape** – general strapping as well as blister padding and securing other dressings.

fig. 9.2 Keep your kit ready for action – but don't forget to air it once in a while.

◎ **Paper & pencil** (waterproof paper is available and a soft pencil will always write no matter what the weather is like) – for recording vital signs and location to save the 'Chinese whispers' that follow an incident.

◎ **Anti-inflammatory & pain relief drugs** (use as directed on package) – Aspirin, Ibuprofen and Paracetamol.

◎ **List of contents** (waterproofed).

fig. 9.3 Changing times – Ken Taylor displays his hunting gear acquired in Greenland (1960). Showing a harpoon, line & rack, shotgun holster, throw stick, sealskin bladder, reversible sealskin mitts (thumbs front and back), tuilik, sealskin boots and dog whip. Photo: Duncan Winning.

ADDITIONAL CONTENTS FOR EXPEDITIONING

◎ **Some means of sterilising water** (could be stove and pot or chemical sterilisation method) – there is no need to boil water for ten minutes for it to become sterile, just bring to the boil then keep covered.

◎ **Sterile needles & syringe**

◎ **Temporary dental fillings** (sugarfree gum works well until you can get to your dentist, it can also hold a crown in place).

◎ **Adrenaline injection** (EPI pen) – for severe allergic reactions.

◎ **Alcohol wipes**

◎ **Antifungal cream**

◎ **Anti-inflammatory**, e.g. Ibuprofen or Diclofenac.

◎ **Aspirin** – for pain and fever.

◎ **Lomotil/Imodium** – for temporarily blocking diarrhoea.

◎ **Paracetamol** – for pain, fever and inflammation.

◎ **Codeine** – for mild to moderate pain and cough.

◎ **Ear drops**

◎ **Erythromycin** (antibiotic for most infections. Suitable for people allergic to penicillin).

◎ **Eye ointment**

◎ **Hydrocortisone cream** – used for chaffing, salt sores and 'nappy rash'.

◎ **Local anaesthetic cream** or lozenges for the mouth and throat.

◎ **Thermometer**

◎ **Valium** (relaxant) – can be useful in shoulder reductions if you are experienced in a suitable method.

◎ **List of contents** (waterproofed) – with doses of drugs and side effects.

The quantities you take of the above drugs will depend directly on the duration and remoteness of your expedition. With the majority of the drugs being available only on prescription, the best idea is to contact your family GP who will advise on the best options for you along with advice on dosage and length of treatment based on illness.

9.2 REPAIR KIT

My repair kit lives in a medium size BDH bottle although any waterproof container or bag is suitable. I have found that dry bags, when used for keeping repair materials in, become damaged easily due to the sharp items within. A rubber seal around the neck of the bottle helps keep the contents drier. Total weight of this is around 1kg.

◎ **Assorted tools** (Allen key, multi-tool, saw etc.) – I carry a hacksaw blade which can be used with some duct tape wrapped around to make a handle. Allen keys of suitable size for all fittings on your kayak and associated equipment. A multi-tool is handy because there are lots of different tools contained within a small size. Screwdrivers should be of a suitable size to allow tightening of any of the screws on your kayak and the ability to fit into your container.

◎ **Copper wire** – for serious stitching.

◎ **Duct tape** (gaffer tape/canoe tape).

◎ **Epoxy putty** – used for more substantial repairs and can be applied when wet, requires kneading by hand so a pair of surgical gloves might be a handy addition.

◎ **Neoprene adhesive**

◎ **Plumber's tape** (Denso tape is great for general temporary repairs, it is a cloth tape impregnated with a horrible green gunge that sticks to everything).

◎ **Flash Band** – supplied for guttering repairs, this is a bitumen backed foil strip that provides substance to a repair. If heated with your hand it can melt slightly allowing a better bond.

◎ **Self-amalgamating tape**

◎ **Sewing kit**

◎ **Sheet of flexible plastic** (cut from soft drinks bottle) – for larger hole reinforcement.

◎ **Spare skeg/rudder wire** and the knowledge of how to replace it.

◎ **Spinnaker tape** (a self-adhesive ripstop nylon, usually sold in 5cm widths on a roll of 4m) – useful for patching tents, paddling tops and many other clothing items. If two pieces are placed on either side of the damaged area then rubbed briskly, the heat created bonds the adhesive through the material giving a stronger repair.

◎ **Two-part epoxy adhesive** – general gluing uses where flexibility is not required.

ADDITIONAL CONTENTS FOR EXPEDITIONING

◎ **Drill bit** (3mm) – it is possible to rotate a drill bit between your index finger and thumb although a small screwdriver might well do the job with less effort.

◎ **Patches of neoprene & nylon**

◎ **Resin, catalyst & matting** – for larger repairs (available from automotive stores; weight around 500 grams).

◎ **Selection of screws & nuts**

9.3 FLARES

There are three basic types of flare available: smoke flare (daytime use), pinpoint flare (night) and parachute flare. Distress flares are coloured red and smoke flares orange; white flares are used for collision warning or illuminating an area for search and rescue purposes.

Parachute flare – The parachute flare is probably the first flare you would use, this fires a rocket to about 300m, which then burns a bright red flare for about sixty seconds that descends slowly by parachute to the sea. If you are in conditions of low cloud or are under a high cliff the possibility of your flare being ineffective is great.

Pinpoint – A pinpoint flare would be your next choice at night. When you spot your would-be rescuer, set off this flare on the downwind side of the kayak and hold it at arm's length. This type of flare gets very hot, the metal tube enclosing the magnesium will glow red due to the intense heat. It will burn for approximately sixty seconds.

Smoke – Smoke flares are used when a rescuer is close during the day. Again set this off on the downwind side of the kayak, this time the flare does not get particularly hot but the smoke smells and tastes foul, it also stains everything it comes in contact with. The smoke produced is very dense and the burn time is roughly sixty seconds.

fig. 9.4 *Top left to right: mini-flares, parachute flare, red pinpoint flare, orange smoke flare, mini rocket flare. Bottom left: waterproof, combined red pinpoint and orange smoke flare.*

9.4 ESSENTIALS

Flares – A good arsenal of flares for a typical sea kayaker would be one each of the above. In addition there are compact mini-flare kits available that have either six or eight shells that fire about 80m into the air. These have proved to be successful, more due to the bang than the red light produced.

Most flares now have a waterproof housing, this allows them to withstand splashes (but not submerging completely) for weeks on end. A good idea is to keep your flares on deck in a waterproof bag, which is tied securely to the kayak.

Carrying flares does not guarantee rescue, as they have to be seen by at least one person who just happens to be looking towards you. Make sure that you know how to operate each and every flare you carry. Know which end is 'live' and know how each is fired. It is also a good idea to be able to do this in the dark or with your eyes closed.

Compass – For most of the kayaking that you do a simple orienteering type hand-held compass will suffice. It is also used when working out distances and bearings from your chart. However, a deck-mounted compass is invaluable if you are likely to be carrying out any type of open crossing. These, however, are expensive and vulnerable to damage. There are several types available, with the choice being that of economics as well as the size of the numerals. The mounting position is critical; if it is too close to you the constant looking down will, more than likely, leave you feeling queasy. Too far away and you will struggle to read the degrees. Somewhere around the front hatch would appear to be the optimum position for most paddlers.

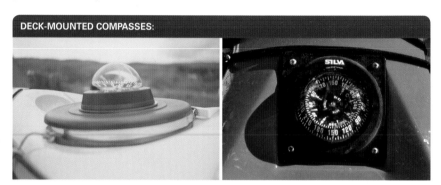

figs. 9.5-6 A retrofit hatch-mounted compass (left) and bow deck-mounted compass in a moulded recess.

Pump – Although a sponge or a bailer is a reasonable way to remove water from a kayak neither is entirely practical whilst at sea, a pump can be more efficient, quicker and harder to lose. Perhaps the simplest is the stirrup type, which is held and operated like a bicycle pump. These are cheap and portable but the major drawback is that both hands are used when emptying your boat. A sensible addition is a flotation collar, as most do not float.

Most kayak manufacturers offer a pump that can be either deck-mounted or fitted inside the kayak on the front bulkhead. For a front deck-mounted pump a detachable handle, tied to the kayak, enables a back and forth movement. This is probably the most effective hand-operated pump as it is possible to pump whilst holding onto your paddle.

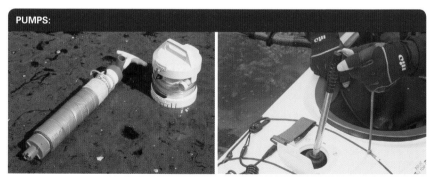

figs. 9.7-8 Stirrup pump and electric pump (left) and a deck-mounted pump (right), the detachable handle is often located in a recess on the deck.

Pumps fitted to the rear deck were the norm until a few years ago. One drawback was that it was virtually impossible to operate by yourself and if you asked a friend they were likely to get soaked by the contents of your kayak.

Bulkhead mounted pumps mean that you can paddle and support whilst emptying your kayak but can feel a bit like rubbing your stomach and patting your head at the same time. One drawback is that when your cockpit area is full of water your exertions are likely to be less than efficient due to you slopping back and forward.

Electrically operated pumps have been around for a while but have not really caught on due to their weight and battery life. They can however remove a large amount of water easily and if the spraydeck is replaced it is possible to paddle whilst the kayak is emptying.

Paddle leashes – I am not a fan of paddle leashes as they can get in the way when performing rescues and self-rescues. However, they can be useful at times. As with any piece of string, make sure you have a knife handy just in case you need to cut it loose.

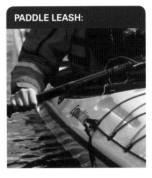

fig. 9.9
Paddle leash.

Of two incidents that have happened to me while trying out a leash, one was funny and the other potentially lethal: Swimming in a big tide race on the west coast of Scotland playing with some ideas on self-rescue, I had decided to try out a paddle leash. The paddle was left to float by itself and because I knew it was attached I could forget about it until needed. As there was a strong wind blowing against the tide I was drifting with the tide and the paddle with the wind. One blade caught in the water and the paddle did a somersault with the other blade hitting the back of my head. As I was paddling alone I did not know what had happened until I saw it start its arc towards my skull again. The other incident involved my neck being wrapped in a friend's leash in breaking waves – not good!

A final piece of equipment every paddler should make for themselves – a checklist of everything they would normally carry.

PLATE XIV *Pastel clouds over Uvkuvissaat, North West Greenland.*
At this lunch spot we were twenty-five nautical miles from the nearest habitation.

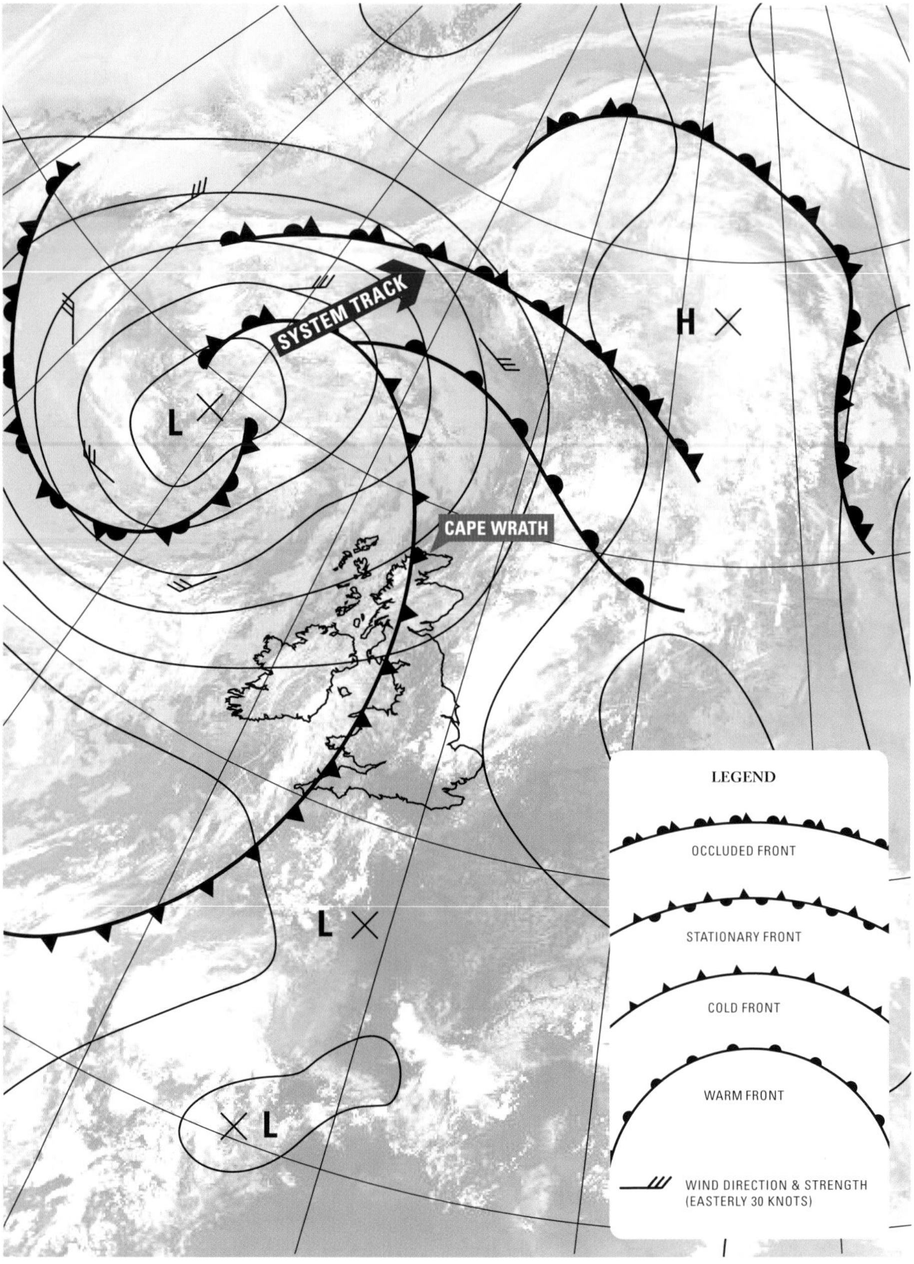

SYSTEM TRACK

CAPE WRATH

H ✕

L ✕

L ✕

✕ L

LEGEND

OCCLUDED FRONT

STATIONARY FRONT

COLD FRONT

WARM FRONT

WIND DIRECTION & STRENGTH
(EASTERLY 30 KNOTS)

fig. 10.1 *A depression passes northward of the British Isles. If you were stood at Cape Wrath, the tip of Scotland facing north the wind would have been south-easterly as the warm front passed overhead with the wind backing to south-westerly as the cold front comes across. With the wind behind you the low will be to your left and the high to your right, as stated by Buys-Ballot's Law.*

10 Weather

Depressions can be very large, sometimes covering many thousands of square miles. Our kayaks are very small and move slowly. A weather system that is moving slowly is probably moving five times faster than we are able to paddle. As sea kayakers, we have to be able to take the big picture and somehow relate this to our immediate area, which for a normal day's paddling is around fifty square miles. It is very easy to lose sight of this when checking the weather – it is almost as easy to blame the weather reporter for getting it wrong.

Weather, as we know it, is the direct consequence of changes in temperature within the moist dense air mass that surrounds the earth. Radiant energy from the sun heats the surface unevenly, warming the atmosphere in some places more than in others. As warm air is less dense than cold air it rises, colder air sinking to replace it. This results in regions of comparatively high pressure neighbouring areas of lower pressure.

Air moves from a high-pressure area to an area of low pressure, but not directly. This movement is deflected by the earth's rotation (Coriolis effect). The resulting flow of air is felt as wind whenever there is a variation in atmospheric pressure between two areas. The strength of the wind is determined by the rate of change of pressure between the two centres. Variation in barometric pressure is one of our principle indications of imminent changes to wind and weather in the local area.

10.1 HIGHS & LOWS

Anticyclones (highs) and depressions (lows) are the major weather systems of the middle latitudes. In the northern hemisphere an anticyclone is a system where wind blows in a clockwise direction around the area of high pressure. At the centre of the high the wind is light or non-existent, this increases progressively and the wind blows at its strongest at the periphery. Our fair weather friends, anticyclones give us reasonably clear skies and moderate winds, in general they move slowly, perhaps even lingering for a few days.

Depressions and their allied frontal systems are mostly responsible for heavy rainfall, strong winds and generally unsettled conditions. In the northern hemisphere the winds blow in an anticlockwise direction around an area of low pressure. These lows vary significantly in extent and intensity – they can track swiftly in any direction but predominantly eastward. The speed that a typical depression would move at is around fifteen to twenty five knots. One that is moving 'slowly' would be travelling at less than fifteen knots. At the opposite end of the scale, a weather system that is moving 'very rapidly' tracks at speeds greater than forty-five knots.

figs. 10.2 A-E
Development of
an occluded front.

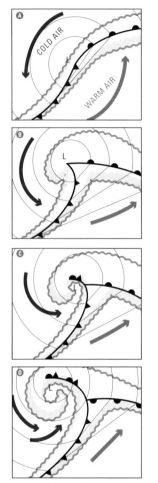

10.2 FRONTS

A front is the leading edge of a mass of air of differing density to the air in front of it. The major air masses that shape British weather are the Polar and Sub-tropical Highs. These vast bodies of air are named according to their geographic source and are of uniform humidity and temperature. Weather systems generated by these air masses may arrive by differing routes – their properties will be dependent on their path. Weather systems generated or passing through the Arctic and Polar regions will be cold – those from tropical regions will be warm – those from maritime regions will be humid and those from continental regions will be dry. Thus a weather system formed by the Polar Front and passing over the North Atlantic will be both cold and humid.

The majority of depressions that move towards Britain assemble along the Polar Front – as the name suggests this is the boundary between two air masses, cold polar air and warm tropical air. As anticlockwise rotation commences (in the northern hemisphere) the pressure drops, a wave forms and a low centre develops. The fronts form and move anticlockwise around the low. The whole system tracks east-north-east with the warm front leading and cold front following. An occluded front occurs when the faster moving cold front catches up with and overtakes the warm front. The occlusion is said to be completed when the warm and cold fronts have come together along their whole length, the low then weakens and drifts north.

fig. 10.3 Cumulonimbus clouds with attendant squall mark
the passage of this cold front. The cold air brings dramatically
improved visibility. ©iStockphoto.com / Vasko Miokovic

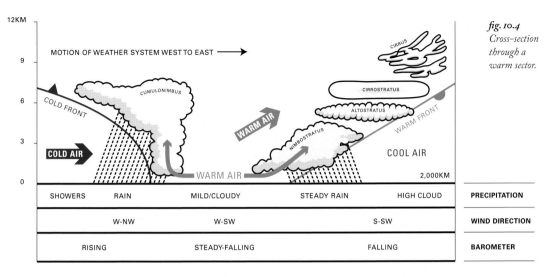

fig. 10.4
Cross-section through a warm sector.

10.3 FRONTAL WEATHER SYSTEMS

It is always a good idea to know where the centre of an approaching low is in relation to your position as the most turbulent winds happen around the centre of the depression.

Buys-Ballot's Law states that if you sit in your kayak with the wind at your back, the centre of the low pressure area will be off to your left (in the northern hemisphere), ie. wind travels anticlockwise around low pressure zones in the northern hemisphere.

Winds above 650 metres blow parallel to the isobars, but surface winds are always 'backed' in relation to the main wind.

Crossed Winds – the 'crossed winds' rule gives a rough guide to weather trends. Face the wind (in the northern hemisphere), look up at the clouds and compare the direction of the higher altitude wind. If the movement is from the right, the weather is likely to deteriorate. If coming from the left, the weather is most likely to improve, but if the movement is directly towards or away from you, the conditions are unlikely to change.

Synoptic Charts – A synoptic chart indicates the distribution of atmospheric pressure throughout an area by means of isobars, these lines are drawn through locations having the same pressure. This forms a pressure contour map similar to a geographical contour map. Closely spaced isobars represent a steep pressure gradient, which produces stronger winds. The arrangement of these isobars gives a good indication of the prevailing weather.

10.4 BACKING & VEERING

In the northern hemisphere a wind is said to 'back' when it changes to blow from a more anticlockwise direction and 'veer' if it changes to blow from a more clockwise direction.

Refer to fig. 10.1, a depression in the North Atlantic, at the start of this chapter.

The warm front is the leading edge of a warm sector – which rides up over the comparatively cold air in front of it. The cold front is the leading edge of a wedge of cold air, which is pushing into the warm sector ahead of it. The depression and its associated fronts are tracking steadily in the general direction of the isobars in the warm sector (north-west).

If you were stood at Cape Wrath looking north, you would probably expect the following sequence of events as the depression passes over.

High cloud from the west increases and lowers as the warm front approaches. The pressure falls, the wind strengthens and backs. Visibility deteriorates and light rain becomes continuous and heavy. As the warm front passes, the pressure will steady and the wind veers. The rain stops or turns to drizzle. In the warm sector visibility is poor with drizzle or showers, wind and pressure remain steady. At the cold front the pressure falls then rises sharply – the wind veers and comes in squalls with heavy rain. As the front moves away the rain stops, visibility improves and the pressure rises.

'Winds becoming cyclonic' is a phrase you will hear often within forecasts. What this indicates is that there will be considerable change in wind direction as a depression tracks across the forecast area.

If you spend a bit of time studying the weather and weather charts, you will soon develop a feel for what is going on. If you know what the pressure system is supposed to be doing and you observe something different, you can alter your own forecast as required.

Keep a weather eye. Look upwind and up weather (where the clouds are coming from). If you are not sure what to look for then look for change. At least you'll know that something is going to happen and eventually through experience you'll be able to tell what.

Weather forecasts have their own language. As you will be using a variety of sources it is worth having a bit of understanding of at least some of the jargon.

METEOROLOGICAL JARGON

SPEED OF WEATHER SYSTEM:

Slowly – less than fifteen knots

Steadily – fifteen to twenty-five knots

Rather quickly – twenty-five to thirty-five knots

Rapidly – thirty-five to forty-five knots

Very rapidly – greater than forty-five knots

PRESSURE TENDENCY:

Rising/falling slowly – change of 0.1 to 1.5 millibars in the preceding three hours.

Rising/falling – change of 1.6 to 3.5 millibars in the preceding three hours.

Rising/falling quickly – change of 3.6 to 6 millibars in the preceding three hours.

Rising/falling very rapidly – change of greater than 6 millibars in the preceding three hours.

Now rising/falling – the pressure has been rising/ falling or steady in the preceding three hours, but was definitely rising/falling at the time of the observation.

VISIBILITY:

Fog – less than half of a nautical mile.

Poor – half to two miles.

Moderate – two to five miles.

Good – more than five miles.

TIMING OF ARRIVAL OF GALE FROM TIME OF ISSUE:

Imminent – less than six hours.

Soon – six to twelve hours.

Later – more than twelve hours.

STRONG WIND WARNINGS:

These are issued, if possible six hours in advance, when winds of Force 6 or more are expected up to five miles offshore and are valid for twelve hours.

A gale warning remains in force until it is amended or cancelled. If the wind speed remains the same for more than twenty-four hours the warning is re-issued.

BEAUFORT SCALE

The other piece of information that is important for us is the Beaufort Scale (see fig. 7.4, limit of adequate reserve). Starting at Force 1 and going to Force 12, the scale is a useful guide to what conditions we might expect to find while on the water. In forecast terminology words are used for winds of Force 8 or above.

Gale – Force 8
(34–40kn or gusts reaching 43–51kn).

Severe Gale – Force 9
(41–47 kn or gusts reaching 52–60kn).

Storm – Force 10
(48–55kn or gusts reaching 61–68kn).

Violent Storm – Force 11
(56–63kn or gusts of 69kn or more).

Hurricane – Force 12 (64kn or more).

10.5 WHETHER THE WEATHER

Whether you are planning to go surfing, expeditioning, exploring or rockhopping round your favourite headland, weather has an effect on everything you do on the sea. It is as well to remember that forecasters on the television and within the weather centres we obtain our reports from have spent several years studying weather patterns and synoptic charts and they can only get it right sometimes. If you are able to see what is happening in the near vicinity of your paddling location you will be able to start predicting the small changes yourself. For an armchair overview you'll find some useful web addresses for weather sites in the selected bibliography.

BEAUFORT SCALE 1-8:

fig. 10.5 Examples of paddling conditions in winds of Beaufort 1 to 8. Force 8 being the limit of feasible paddling.

SURVIVAL PADDLING
SEEK SHELTER ON LAND IMMEDIATELY

PLATE XV *West coast of Mingulay during spell of high pressure, cirrostratus clouds causing shielding of the sun.*

PLATE XVI *A stiff offshore breeze steepens the face of the surf waves. Pease Bay, Scotland.*
Photo: Douglas Wilcox

11 Strong Winds

A long time ago I was paddling to meet up with some friends and set off from Fairlie just south of Largs. The wind was Force 6 gusting 7 and there was a swell of around two and a half metres running. I put on my personal stereo, cranked up the volume and set off. I was heading to the south end of the Isle of Bute and after crossing Millport Bay took a transit on the point I aimed to arrive at. I can remember well the tune that was playing; Queen, Another One Bites the Dust. This is a fantastic rhythm to paddle to and only slightly ironic that I failed to see or hear a racing dingy flying towards me from the rear quarter. It and its crew passed within three metres of me and probably had no idea that I was there. I have never used a personal stereo on the water since!

Paddling into strong winds can have a similar effect; it is not unusual to find yourself in front of a fishing boat not knowing that it is closing on you quickly. It is always good practice to have a look over your shoulder every now and again to make sure you are not about to be run down.

A strong wind causes many things to happen, one of the benefits is that there is a wind 'shadow' downwind of the wave. What this means is that when you are paddling in big conditions there are equal periods of stronger and weaker wind. Use the less windy areas to make any changes in direction if the wind is too strong and perhaps grabbing at your paddle on the top of the wave. The converse of this is that the worst conditions for weathercocking are when you have a strong beam wind coming off low-lying land. There is no fetch, no waves and no wind shadow to lessen the effect.

When coming from the sheltered area behind an island or rock into a strong wind, there is a similar effect as if you were paddling in tide. As the wind squeezes around the rock you have been sheltered behind, its velocity will increase by a substantial amount. A good idea is to think about edging before you find the bow being turned downwind. The biggest difference is that you will tend to be blown over towards your downwind side rather than in the tide where you would flip upstream.

11.1 DOWNDRAUGHTS, KATABATIC WINDS & WILLIWAWS

When you are paddling in the shelter of cliffs beware of the danger of downdraughts. The higher the cliff the stronger the wind is likely to be. These ferocious winds can hit you without notice, splitting up your group and causing absolute chaos.

Generally if the wind is Force 6 or above there starts to be noticeable effects of the wind accelerating in a downward direction. When you are close to the cliff the local wind can seem to be coming from the sea and not from the direction of the main wind. If you are in just the right (or wrong) place the wind will be coming at you from above, flattening everything and fanning out from the centre of impact. If you happen to be on the outside of this type of wind you will find that it is not at all constant but varies in gusts, some of which are stronger but many are a good deal weaker than the main wind.

fig. 11.1 Downdraught off St Kilda.

Downdraughts may be brought about or exacerbated by the effects of katabatic or föhn winds (winds which descend a hill, mountain or glacier). A common form of cold air katabatic wind often takes place shortly after sunset as the land cools and the air above becomes denser and starts to descend. The winds produced can be ferocious and are accelerated as they are funnelled down valleys towards the sea, catching those who have set out to sea on a calm evening unawares. These local winds may blow up to gale force for an hour or so before dying away.

The Alaskan word for a sudden blast of katabatic is a Williwaw, particularly those off the Aleutian Islands. Many such winds have earned names of their own across the globe, such as the Pittaraq (a Greenland North Westerley descending from the ice cap).

Föhn is generally the term for kabatic winds which are warmer and drier than their surroundings, where wind forced over a mountain range has caused water vapour to condense and precipitate on the windward side and peak, leading to warming of the drier air as it descends the leeward side. This effect can cause desertification in some regions and assist glaciation in others.

11.2 ROLLING IN A STRONG WIND

Rolling in a strong wind can be quite different to rolling elsewhere. If the wind is above Force 6 chances are that you will not be able to get all the way upright when rolling on the downwind side. As you will be blown across the surface of the water, rolling on the upwind side will require less effort. If you come up on the upwind side and convert the roll into a low brace immediately on surfacing you are less likely to fall over again.

Rolling on the downwind side the boat will be pushed towards the paddle and the paddle will have a tendency to dive. This is one of the rare occasions to use a sculling support, until either the gust that knocked you in subsides, or you can get a breath and capsize to roll on the other side.

PLATE XVII *If you can see what is written on the surface of the water, it is possible to determine hazards as well as safe areas.*

12 Reading the Water

Reading the water is a skill, which like all others needs to be practised for it to work for you when you need it. In areas of turbulence the water seems to have a mind of its own and there appears to be no structure or regularity to the movement. There are a few generalisations that can make things a bit easier to understand.

- ◎ In shallow water or around rocks, water which is dark coloured moves up and down. Conversely, water which is aerated and lighter in colour is flowing somewhere (up, down, left, right or around and around). Dark coloured water is generally the safest place to be.

- ◎ When picking your way through a rock garden, look for the dark, deep water and keep an eye out for any patches of white that encroach into your chosen channel. These will push and pull you from side to side and any attempt at a draw will be pretty much ineffectual.

- ◎ When you have exhausted all possibilities of landing in a sheltered area and simply have to come ashore through big waves, look for areas of weakness. Dark coloured water, reefs to hide behind, slightly lower wave peaks due to deeper water – scout what lies ahead from the crest of the wave and be prepared to back paddle retreat from an area that you don't like the look of.

- ◎ Rips* are often safe areas for sea kayaks to get in through surf, look for a stream that flows into a bay, chances are that is where the rip will be. If there is no stream then your best bet is around the sides of the bay if the waves are coming in squarely, however, here there will generally be quite a bit of turbulence around the rocks.

- ◎ Dumping surf can cause a few problems. Easy to see from land these waves keep most of their power until they fall to the beach. When you are paddling towards a coastline with swell running onto it, there are some indications that there is likely to be dumping surf. Generally there is only one line of breaking waves and the wavelength does not shorten much as it nears the shore.

* **rip**, an area of water flowing back out to sea. As waves wash ashore, the water deposited creates its own way back out beyond the waves; in these areas the waves are deadened and often much lower than the surrounding water.

◎ The amount of air escaping from the collapsed wave is indicative of the amount of power released. A more explosive break is dissipating its energy much faster than a less explosive one.

◎ When an isolated rock or reef has an occasional dumping wave break onto it, it is known as a 'boomer'. What happens is that the water pulls away from the reef, exposing the top, then the next wave arrives and the crest explodes onto the bare rock. This is probably the worst place you could be with your kayak.

◎ Glance at the horizon, this will give you an idea of what conditions are like farther out. You can normally see large waves from over three miles away (especially overfalls).

◎ Always assume there will be much rougher water off a headland. This is because of the effect of the seabed on waves. In tidal areas the flow will be faster and rougher off the point than to either side.

◎ In a fast inshore tidal flow there are always eddies that you can use in a sea kayak, these are not detailed in nautical publications as most craft have deeper draught than a kayak.

◎ Big mushrooming boils of water indicate an uneven sea floor and are the consequence of water being pushed up from deeper areas to the surface. These present little obstacle to a sea kayak but can be disconcerting when first encountered. The water flows upwards from the centre and outwards.

◎ Water being blown through a constriction creates a current. High winds can also back up a tidal effect, increasing or dampening it.

◎ When the wind blows against the direction of the tide the waves will increase in height, steepen and possibly break depending on the strength of both. The opposite happens when both wind and tide are moving in the same direction, the wave height will decrease and the distance between successive crests will increase.

fig. 12.1 Subtle effects of wind and tide off the cliffs of Eshaness, Shetland.

The local effects of wind on water can be difficult to read, but revealing. When you look from land to the sea you can sometimes see silver and grey lines on the surface of the water, what is happening is the wind is opposing the tidal flow. The wind does not need to be strong and neither does the tide, in fact, the effect can be seen more clearly with light winds and weak tides. You can use these lines to ensure you are going with the flow, the assistance may not be great but it is much better to be in your favour than against you. When the wind and tide are both stronger the appearance of these lines is much less distinct A momentary 'cat's paw' effect of a breeze over the water can accentuate an area of disturbance.

When the wind gusts you will see patches of darker water. As these approach, you will feel the wind increase gradually until it is at its full strength. You should also be able to see when the gust is nearing its end, as the water will revert to its original texture.

A squall is a highly localised, brief but fierce wind. As with a gust, when a squall is about to arrive there will be a darkening of the surface of the water. This time however, instead of an irregular patch, the dark water forms a line. This line often indicates the arrival of the wedge of cold air in a cold front. Called a line squall for obvious reasons, the wind within it is travelling substantially faster than the general wind. As the line squall hits, you will find that the wind has veered (changed direction clockwise, eg. from south-west to west). If this squall is very strong, not only will there be the veering wind but the water will be thrown into the air causing a lot of spray.

The fiercest squalls I have been in were on the west coast of Scotland. A friend and I had been paddling around Islay and the wind had been very strong all week. We left our camp after listening to the shipping forecast.

On the water we were in the lee of the land although the wind was strong. Rounding the north west point, Rubha a' Mhàil, we saw the first of the squalls approach. The wind was accelerating down the slopes of the Paps of Jura. We paddled hard towards the line knowing that we were now on the exposed shore and not knowing how long the squall might last.

Just before the full force of the wind hit us the spray lifted from the water was about one metre high, and we were less than ten metres apart. I do not know what my companion did but all I could do was to brace into the wind, keeping low over the front deck with the back of my head turned into the wind. When this first blast had dissipated, despite our best efforts we were now more than five hundred metres apart. We still had around four miles of paddling until we could land and there was no let-up in the wind. The squalls came about every fifteen to twenty minutes during our race to shelter. Exhausted, we were finally reunited at our destination.

After pulling the boats well above the high water line and tying them down I found a camping spot, pitched the tent, then made and ate our meal. At this point I realised that my buddy was nowhere to be seen, so I headed to the hotel. When I arrived, he was settled into a comfy chair with a beer in his hand. He had already had a bath and a meal. The night we passed at the pub is another story!

PLATE XVIII *Duncan Winning crossing a fjord in North West Greenland, five miles from the glacier.*

PLATE XIX *Crenellations line the battlements of this castle of ice,*
likely to be a recently separated portion of ice–sheet.

PLATE XX *Icebergs on a platinum sea, North West Greenland.*

13 Method for Approximately Grading the Sea (MAGS)

Whitewater kayakers have developed a system for classifying the severity of the river or rapid based on flow, obstructions and gradient. Ranging from one to six this subjective scale is only an indication of conditions you are likely to come across. As sea kayakers we need a system that can accommodate the changeable nature of the ocean and yet be familiar enough to indicate the skill level required. Below is a method adapted from original work by Eric Soares[†].

When you use the process ensure you account for the worst conditions you are likely to encounter. There is no measure for freak conditions.

Rate the ten factors in turn using realistic estimates; add the scores together and divide the total by twenty. The result is the relative grade of water. Any adjusted total of 1.9 and below is Grade I. Above that the grade of water is the first number in the total, eg. 3.8 = Grade 3 and 5.4 = Grade 5. Above 6, the numbers are immaterial; it is very difficult, heavy water.

I	II	III	IV	V	VI	GRADE
Easy	Moderate	Intermediate	Advanced	Extreme	Very extreme	**DESCRIPTION**
Little danger	Small seas, very easy terrain	Regular seas, easy landing areas	Confused seas, difficult landing areas	Heavy water, very confused seas	V. heavy water, completely unpredictable	**DIFFICULTY**
Very little chance of injury	Little chance of injury	Chance of injury – reliable roll required	Injury likely during an incident	Serious injury or loss of life possible	Loss of life highly likely in the event of an accident	**RISK**

† *Extreme Sea Kayaking*, Eric Soares & Michael Powers, Ragged Mountain Press (1999)

FACTORS TO CONSIDER WHEN APPLYING MAGS

❶ **Water temperature.** 20°C is a comfortable temperature for swimming with no protective clothing. Subtract the actual temperature from twenty and multiply by two. The result is the score. (Obviously a thermometer will give an accurate reading but there is data available on mean sea temperatures in various publications).

❷ **Wind speed.** Comparable to the speed of a river. The score is the same as the wind speed in knots.

❸ **Wave height.** Take the average wave height. Each metre scores six (30cm scores two).

❹ **Swimming to safety.** Each 100m scores one point, up to a maximum twenty. Give twenty if on an open crossing (more than two nautical miles), or close to cliffs where there is no escape.

❺ **Breaking waves.** In shallow water give thirty points if there are breaking waves over 60cm high.

❻ **Rockhopping.** Score twenty if you are planning to participate.

❼ **Sea caves.** As for rockhopping, score twenty if you are going in.

❽ **Night.** Scores an automatic twenty.

❾ **Fog.** Scores up to a maximum of twenty for dense fog.

❿ **Additional hazards.** This is where your knowledge of the sea comes in. Score a minimum of ten for each eventuality not covered within the table. (Shipping, tidal flow, rip current, other water users etc.)

Rate the ten factors in turn using realistic estimates; add the scores together and divide the total by twenty.

Note that the first four factors apply whenever you are on the sea, and each factor has been weighted depending on the severity of the risk. Also remember that this method of grading the sea is only an estimate and in no way should replace the knowledge gained by time spent on the water in a variety of conditions. It does not take other paddlers into account although this could be factored in under number ten. Finally, as river kayakers have 'chicken runs' so do we. The relative grade works when you are actually in the conditions you have accounted for, not when paddling close to them.

FACTOR #	NAME	POINTS	SCORE
1	Water Temperature	2 points for each degree below 20°C.	
2	Wind Speed	1 point per knot of wind speed.	
3	Wave Height	6 points per metre of vertical wave height.	
4	Swim Distance to Safety	1 point per 100m up to a maximum of 20.	
5	Breaking Waves	30 points – waves breaking in shallow water.	
6	Rockhopping	20 points if paddling in rocks.	
7	Sea Cave	20 points if entering sea caves.	
8	Night	20 points if it is night time.	
9	Fog	Up to 20 points if present.	
10	Miscellaneous	10 points or more for each additional danger.	
		Divide total by 20 to give grade of water	

fig. 13.1 Sea ice starts to form at a water temperature of minus 1.8°C, although icebergs have been found at latitudes as low as 48° N (that's farther south than the Channel Islands!)

PLATE XXI *Big arch, Strathy Point, north coast of Scotland.*

14 Caves

Caves are special places to explore and are generally spectacular; there are however a few things worth considering before venturing inside…

Most of the caves that I have been in are caused by intrusive dykes. On Skye there are uncountable basalt intrusions created by prehistoric volcanic activity on the island itself, on Rum, which is the closest southern neighbour, and on Mull, about thirty miles south. These wave-battered fault lines are the weakness in the rock where the erosion forms the cave. The same forces that shaped the cave in the first place (swell and wave action) are also the providers of most of your excitement.

If you have never been into a particular cave before then it is best to go in carefully when there is no swell. If there is any swell entering the cave it is generally a sensible idea to reverse in. This means that you can see bigger waves coming and you are in a better position to paddle back out if it looks like it is going to get horrible. Imagine doing a spot of rockhopping in the complete dark and you are getting close to the feeling of being in a cave with swell. If the cave is wide and open there is little to concern you but if it is a long narrowing funnel then things will start to get quite exciting even with a minimal swell. One thing that is guaranteed is that any wave action will pick you up and turn you round only to dump you unceremoniously onto the sharpest, most awkward rock. If you are in a particularly large cavern, the sound effects and monster gurgling noises are very disconcerting especially if you are a long way from the entrance.

If there is any swell entering the cave it is generally a sensible idea to reverse in.

Hearing replaces sight as your primary sense. When you go into a cave, listen behind you for any sounds. A negligible swell on a beach can create a one metre wave in a narrow channel and, depending on the depth of water in the cave, can break. Keep looking behind you as you go deeper and don't get too frantic when the light is blocked by the swell coming in through a narrow entrance.

If you are facing out to sea, you can get a feel for the power that caused the cave in the first place. Also you can see the bigger waves approach. If you see light shine through the wave and it turns the water within to emerald, you can assume that it is pretty big. If the colour disappears from the water it is huge, expect to get a proper beating, try to keep your kayak aligned with the cave walls (forwards or backwards is fine in this instance) and avoid being broached at all costs.

Always ensure there is plenty of headroom within the cave, it is a good idea to look up as well as to the side. If a bigger than average wave comes in, which it will, you will be going up more rapidly than you could begin to imagine.

Some caves have a back entrance; the local paddlers may know about this but it is unlikely that many other water users will have this knowledge. Sometimes it is perfectly safe to enter here and then paddle out through the surging wave at the main entrance.

The noise coming from within the cave is generally a good indicator of what is happening there, get to know what the different sounds mean to you. A hollow boom coming from a distance generally indicates a lower area towards the rear of the cave. Hissing suggests escaping air due to a narrowing in the passage with there being a reduced ceiling height as well. General gurgling and whitewater type noise is generally an indication of a safe cave. Crashing surf suggests… I'll leave it to your imagination.

Remember that a rescue is very unlikely to take place within a cave and that if you, or a buddy, do capsize and wet exit, swimming your kayak and paddle out to the entrance may be the only satisfactory answer. Also, as you will be in close proximity to rock and breaking water, you might want to consider a helmet for personal protection before venturing into these subterranean grottos. A head torch is a useful addition.

fig. 14.1 Facing out to sea keeping an eye on the swell, Wiay, West Skye.

PLATE XXII *A big friendly cave, West Skye.*

PLATE XXIII *Paddler about to disappear.*
Photo: Douglas Wilcox

15 **Big Swell**

Big swell paddling is a delight, land appears and disappears, you lose sight of your buddies and they of you; breaking waves seem to appear out of nowhere, lie in wait and explode just as you get really close.

Swell is generally caused by atmospheric conditions, with the wind being the obvious culprit. Friction from the wind interacting with the water causes waves, the longer and stronger the wind the bigger the wave. Swell travels in a straight line away from the area of origination until it reaches an obstacle. The size of a swell can increase or decrease as it interpolates with other swell patterns.

Other phenomena that cause swell are earthquakes, massive landslips and meteorite impacts, each of which may generate tsunami (tidal waves). The power of a tsunami can be truly awesome as observed in the Indian Ocean, December 2004. Caused by an underwater earthquake, the resulting surface wave was only a few centimetres high, but the wave was full-depth (its effect went from the surface to the ocean floor). When it came close to land the first indication was that the water drained from beaches and reefs only to be replaced by a very much larger lump of sea. If you are on the water when a tsunami occurs, the best option for your survival is to turn out to sea and paddle as if your life depended on it, because it probably does.

Check out the chapter on Surf & Surfing for more on forecasting swell. However it is a big subject, so just choose an Internet search engine and type 'swell forecasting'. There are a few addresses in the Further Reading section that I have found useful and interesting.

Most information displayed is primarily for surfers and although you might not be going to surf, you will still benefit from knowing what size of waves are forecast. Remember that, like a weather forecast, predicting waves is not an exact science. If you visit a place often you can build up a picture of what size the swell actually is for any given forecast data.

A nautical chart is because, knowing the depths, you can work out the breaks that are likely to happen given a certain amount of swell. If there is a swell of three metres running and a rock with charted depth of two metres, there is a chance that when the swell meets with the rock there will be a breaking wave formed. Waves start to 'feel' bottom when the depth is around half the wavelength or approximately one and a half times the wave height.

Wave height is the vertical distance from trough to peak of a wave. **Wavelength** is the horizontal distance from a peak to the peak of the next wave. Further explanation is given in the next chapter, Surf & Surfing.

Look well in front of where you are paddling. This will give you reliable information as to what is likely to be happening when you get close to any critical areas. If you also look farther out to sea you will get a feel for any larger than normal swell coming towards you; this will give you a chance to react and change your direction if need be.

15.1 POSITION FIX FROM SWELL CHARACTERISTICS

The wave height and shape of a swell will reveal clues about the local depth of water. Assuming you are using a chart for navigation rather than a topographical map, you can read the sea state and relate this to what you are looking at on paper. For instance, when a shallow area jacks up the swell, you can pinpoint your position fairly easily. This is similar in method to that which a sailor might use when making soundings.

15.2 THE BEHAVIOUR OF WAVES

Reflection - Waves will be reflected by steep shores, cliffs or sea walls. If, like me, you can remember some of the basic physics that our patient teachers tried to infuse our brains with, there may be a recollection of interference patterns and waves – when two wave crests of equal height meet the result is a crest that is twice the height of the original. Furthermore, the angle of reflection is equal to the angle of incidence.

So the reflected waves will interpolate with the incoming waves in a largely predictable and regular pattern (an interference pattern) causing an area of disturbed water where wave heights spike (this can be quite explosive) – expect to find this 'clapotis' anywhere there is a sheer coastline or harbour wall. A headland bluff that is in the path of a swell is probably best given a wide berth. There will however, be a null point quite close to the rock where the water is less chaotic and almost calm compared with the sea around you.

fig. 15.1 Reflected waves can cause explosive clapotis. ©iStockphoto.com / YuriyVZ

Refraction – is a change in the speed of propagation of a wave due to variation in the depth of water in which it is travelling. Where the wave approaches shallow water at an angle or the shallow water is irregular in shape this will result in a bend in the previously parallel and straight waves. This effect explains why waves never break at an angle on a beach, but are refracted toward the beach as it becomes ever more shallow.

Wave height will tend to be focussed on points and reefs, and dissipated into bays and coves. The varied bathymetry of a coastline will produce an assortment of refraction effects along its length. The refraction effect will be stronger the longer the period of the swell, and so too the wave height upon breaking will be greater (than for a shorter period swell of the same height in deep water).

Diffraction – is the bending and interference of waves as they pass an obstruction or gap (normally seen as edge diffraction around a headland). The angle at which the wave is bent is proportional to the wavelength and inversely proportional to the width of the obstruction.

fig. 15.2
Focussing effect of refraction on headlands.

You may take shelter behind an island; if the swell were 100% on the exposed side, a rule of thumb would be that on its sheltered side it would have dropped to 10% of the original height. Unfortunately what also happens is that the bigger waves continue around the island and come together some distance away on the downwind side, resulting in an area of interference where the waves jack up. Sometimes this area is shown on a chart as overfalls, sometimes it is not and only your knowledge of the sea and its moods will predict where, when and how severe the conditions will be. If the island is close in-shore the effect of the interference may not be noticeable at all, due to the added effects of reflection and refraction.

fig. 15.3 *Wave diffraction around an iceberg, creating a regular interference pattern.*

15.3   REEFS

Swell lands on the exposed side of a reef and generally pours over, then off the sheltered side. So when paddling in the shelter of a reef, although you will be paddling against a current flowing from the reef you should have less swell to deal with.

15.4   HARBOURS

Are very obvious safe places from swell. What is important to remember is that there will be a lot of other traffic using these areas. All rules of the road, at least power giving way to sail and sail to human power, go out of the window when there is a big swell setting across the entrance. The best thing to remember is that 'MIGHT HAS RIGHT'. For your own safety ensure you are not in a position which could end up with you and a larger vessel competing for the entrance, you are small enough to manoeuvre and your kayak is much more seaworthy than anything else on the water. Make sure you are in the safest position you can be and that you give way to everything else.

15.5   ESTIMATING HEIGHT OF SWELL & WAVES

Estimating swell and wave height whilst at sea is not a science or even an art, it's sooth-saying. There are many methods written about in equally as many publications – for our purposes it is best to keep things simple.

If you have a distant horizon the waves are less than one metre.

If your horizon is the crest of the wave immediately in front, the waves are over a metre.

Anything bigger than this is only talk for the party afterwards, over one metre and communication within your group becomes difficult. If you are paddling by yourself there is less to concern you, as there is no need to watch out for another kayaker. You do however have to remember to watch out for other water users.

PLATE XXIV *Ensure adequate space between paddlers in swell conditions.*

PLATE XXV *Balance, poise and control.*

16 Surf and Surfing

The surfing of ocean waves is itself a subject of a library of books so here we'll deal with some of the techniques and tactics that are pertinent to the sea kayaker. Forecasting surf producing swells is a reasonable place to start - what is the likelihood of encountering breaking waves (wanted or unwanted), and where will they form?

Imagine being on an expedition somewhere and being unable to obtain a weather forecast by radio. If you had no idea about how the weather develops then you could easily be caught out on an exposed coast with big swell and heavy surf. If however you had a bit of knowledge it would be within the realms of possibility to forecast swell.

When the wind blows over the ocean the friction starts to build waves. The resulting waves increase in size the stronger and the longer the duration this wind blows. If this wind has blown for twenty-four hours the wave height will not increase much more. When the resulting swell has travelled away from their area of origination it is said to be mature. These ocean waves travel at speeds of between fifteen and twenty knots and generally have a wavelength, measured in seconds. The wave 'period' can be between two and twenty five seconds (speed divided by wavelength). For a period of less than ten seconds the waves are likely to be 'wind' waves and greater than ten seconds 'swell' waves.

When you spot a persistent low pressure area over the ocean on your weather map, which has an area of tightly packed isobars (producing a strong wind) you can assume it will be kicking out a swell. As discussed in Chapter 10 a low pressure (in the northern hemisphere) will generate winds in an anticlockwise direction around its centre, along the isobars backed by roughly 20°. The area over which the tightly packed isobars take effect (where the winds blows strongest and longest in one direction) is called the fetch, and the resulting swell will travel away in a straight line roughly 20° to the isobars in this area. If you expect a swell to be heading your way, you can make your calculations about how big it will be and how soon it will reach you from looking at the area of fetch.

The time taken for swell to travel varies greatly depending on many factors: strength of wind, duration, size of fetch as well as other factors to be taken into account such as decay and convergence. Decay is just what it sounds like; the swell slowly reduces in size the further it travels from its source, in much the same way as your voice is less loud the further someone is from you. Convergence is when two or more swells come together to form one larger swell, this is how sets are formed.

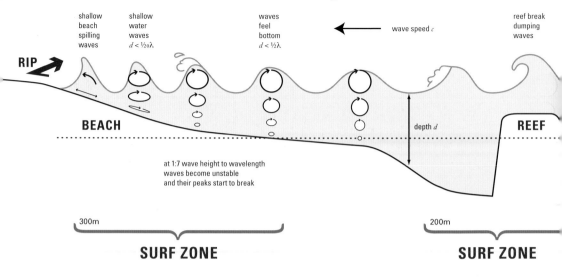

shallow beach spilling waves

shallow water waves $d < \frac{1}{20}\lambda$

waves feel bottom $d < \frac{1}{2}\lambda$

wave speed c

reef break dumping waves

RIP

BEACH

depth d

REEF

at 1:7 wave height to wavelength waves become unstable and their peaks start to break

300m

200m

SURF ZONE

SURF ZONE

16.1 PERSONAL SAFETY

In the surf zone you can expect a high impact experience – so depending on the severity of the conditions, you may well come across the occasional bump to the head, bruising, broken ribs, dislocated shoulders and worst of all, broken kayaks. When surfing, most injuries I have come across have been caused by the bow of a kayak. So if you keep clear of other kayaks and avoid big dumping surf... you'll probably be alright.

The question of whether to wear a helmet or not will always give rise to good debate. If your choice is to always wear one when surfing your sea kayak, what happens when you are on expedition and there just happens to be some surf you have to land or launch through? If you have only ever surfed while wearing a helmet then now might not be the best time to try without. If you weigh up the risks and make a choice based on your experiences, you will most likely find that your skill will improve over time.

It is amazing to watch many paddlers putting on a helmet and going through a person-ality change. Some mild mannered folk become dangerous while others seem to have a do or die mentality.

Remember though that if you are going to be injured it will most likely be one of your friends that has lost control and is heading your way! Surfing in a group when you have five metre kayaks is a sure way of asking for something to happen. Most injuries that I've witnessed have happened when there is an uncontrolled moment close to other kayakers.

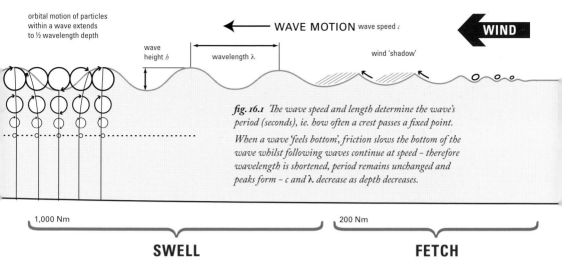

orbital motion of particles
within a wave extends
to ½ wavelength depth

WAVE MOTION wave speed c

WIND

wave
height h

wavelength λ

wind 'shadow'

fig. 16.1 *The wave speed and length determine the wave's period (seconds), ie. how often a crest passes a fixed point.*

When a wave 'feels bottom', friction slows the bottom of the wave whilst following waves continue at speed – therefore wavelength is shortened, period remains unchanged and peaks form – c and λ decrease as depth decreases.

1,000 Nm

200 Nm

SWELL

FETCH

16.2 PADDLING OUT

Watch for a while and then watch some more, you will see that there are sets of waves that come in. A good plan is to be on the water inside of the break, everything in place and ready to paddle immediately after the largest wave has come towards you. Hopefully this will give you plenty of time to get out beyond the critical area. As you paddle forwards make sure that you reach over the crest and plant the paddle on the back of the wave.

If the wave gets to the critical point as you approach, you have three options: the first is to sprint as fast as you are able towards the peak, as you reach the top of the wave throw your weight forwards and bring your knees up sharply. If you are lucky you will become airborne off the back of the wave and land with an almighty thump.

If the wave has already started to crest you are very likely to take a pounding, one way of minimising the abuse your body gets is to align yourself and paddle with the kayak, in a tucked screw-roll type

fig. 16.2 *Reach forward and plant your paddle on the back of the wave.*

position, just as the wave is about to break on you. Assuming you have sufficient forward speed, your kayak, and hopefully you, will pierce the wave and appear out the other side.

The third option is to capsize just before the wave reaches you, wait until it has passed, then roll up and begin your quest for the open sea again.

If you have misjudged the size and power of the wave, you are going to get pretty well beaten up. If you don't back loop as the wave hits you, you will start to back-surf, which will most likely end in a power-flip shoreward. Of course this looks great on your mate's video as well as in the photographs, but as none of our bodies are getting any younger we should take a bit of care of them.

16.3 CATCHING A WAVE

To accelerate a sea kayak from rest to maximum speed takes around eight to ten strokes. Obviously if you wait until the back of your boat is rising on the wave before starting to paddle there is a chance you will miss the wave unless it is just about to break.

If you are close to shore among breaking waves, have your kayak moving forwards and pointing in the general direction of intended travel. As the stern lifts, increase your cadence but keep your shoulders relatively quiet (if you rotate too much the kayak becomes unsettled and can then behave how it wants). When you start to pick up speed ensure your body weight is forward as this allows for maximum rotation when you have caught the wave.

On the open ocean environment (where the waves are less steep), catching a wave is slightly different; if you wait until the back of your kayak has started to lift you will miss most of the waves. A much better option is to put the effort in as a wave has just passed and the bow of your kayak is pointing into the air. You will be going at your maximum speed as the stern is lifted by the next wave and you will now start planing on the face of the wave.

fig. 16.3 Catching a wave from well out back requires a turn of speed to match the wave.

16.4 STAYING ON A WAVE

When paddling a sea kayak, staying on a wave requires control, anticipation, observation, application of skill and a considerable amount of luck.

After the kayak has accelerated down the wave what do you do? It is now probably too late to try to recover and start any turn as all planing will have stopped and the rear of the boat appears to be fixed on rails. Watch most sea kayakers and you will see them lean way back in the boat and stern rudder as far back as they can get, unfortunately all this succeeds in doing is to lock the stern into its track even more.

A better option is to stay high on the wave, lean forwards and keep the kayak on edge, ruddering or even braking on alternate sides. This means that you keep position much higher on the wave and the kayak will not slide into the trough where it is almost impossible to recover from. Start turning early with your body leading the way; keep your weight forward and look where you want to end up.

Torque turn – to hold your position at the top of a wave it will be necessary, due to the absolute hull speed, to 'torque' on alternate sides when you are at the crest, this effectively slows the kayak and turns it towards the side the stroke is performed on. In this position, at the top of the wave, the kayak will turn very quickly due to there being less of it in the water. Prepare to initiate a turn on the other side as soon as the kayak has started to rotate.

The torque is a more dynamic stroke than the rudder and consists of a small part of a reverse sweep carried out towards the end of the first segment of the arc. If you pre-rotate your shoulders to face where you want the kayak to be after the turn is complete you will be able to engage all of your

fig. 16.4 A paddler using torque to hold his position on the top of the wave.
Photo: Les Wilson

largest muscle groups. Torque is defined as 'force applied at a distance from the centre of rotation'. The centre of rotation of a sea kayak when it is on the top of a wave is around the cockpit area. The force you apply starts with the paddle blade and finishes with your feet.

With your kayak on the top of the wave in the broken water, keep your elbows slightly bent and locked, this allows you to transfer the maximum pressure to the paddle blade. Edge and rotate towards the paddle side and plant the blade without reaching behind you. By using the force of water acting on the back of the blade you can now move your kayak with your legs, stomach and back muscles. If you push with your hand which is nearest the working blade and at the same time pull with the other you will be imparting maximum effort to the blade. As before, balance, poise and control are the key to performance.

If travelling diagonally on the wave the bow of the kayak will most likely be in the air, this is fine as long as it stays there. Unfortunately what tends to happen is that the bow will drop especially when you remember to get your weight forwards. The result of this is that the bow stops in the dead water while the rest of the kayak and you are still travelling towards the beach at great speed. It looks fast and powerful and that is because it is! The chances are that you will land on the down wave shoulder; this in itself is not a problem, however, if you were to try a support stroke on this side there is a high chance of catastrophic damage being done to your shoulder joint. If you find yourself in this position, the best option is to get forward into a tucked roll position keeping a good hold on your paddle. All of your stray body parts will be better protected like this and as a bonus you will be in a better position to think about rolling after the wave has passed.

When you have been flipped by the wave in this manner a roll is an easy proposition. Assuming that you are able to roll reasonably proficiently, it is a simple case of extending your forward hand until it is in a protected high brace position (elbows and chin low). Due to the motion of water particles within the wave, your blade will be in the uprising flow which means that you will only have to hold onto the paddle and be prepared to keep bracing into the wave when you return to the upright position. However, the chances are that you will be power flipped again unless most of the power has dissipated from the wave.

16.5 GETTING OFF A WAVE

EARLY TURN:

By turning to face back out to sea before the wave has broken onto you, you should be able to control your rate of progress towards the beach. This requires you to be able to turn whenever you need to rather than only when you can.

BOW STALL:

Stalling is a good way to get off the wave if you are able to control your speed and direction and the waves are a suitable size. Keep high on the wave and wait until it is about to break. Line the bow up to be perpendicular to the wave face, then aim to bury the front of the boat with your weight forwards. As soon as the bow engages, shift your weight back and stand on the footrest. The bow should be in the dead water in the trough and the whitewater will flow past the hull. If you have enough time while the kayak is stalled, try to initiate a vertical spin, this will allow you to be facing back out to sea and ready for the next wave.

fig. 16.5 The more you put into your edging and leaning, the more you will get out of it.

CAPSIZE, WAIT & ROLL:

This takes a lot of courage and very well sealed nostrils. You will get your sinuses flushed out, not only with water but most likely there will be a considerable amount of sand in there too. When your run has ceased to be viable just go for it! Hang around until you are sure the crest has gone over you and then roll. You should have just enough time to gather your thoughts and get a breath before repeating again.

SWIM FOR IT:

If you do end up swimming, make sure that you are on the seaward end of your kayak and holding onto it with a death grip. The boat will pull you towards the beach much faster than you are able to swim; it is also very buoyant and can support you when you tire.

BACK PADDLE TO CONTROL LANDING:

Back paddling on the face of the wave allows a controlled landing. When a wave starts to lift the stern, reverse paddle until the back of the boat drops onto the back face of the wave. Now paddle forwards on the back face of the wave until you feel the back of your kayak being lifted again (just the opposite of catching a wave).

Assuming that you are able to get into a position that will allow you to catch some waves, stop and think for a moment… ask yourself these questions and if you can truthfully answer each one positively, consider the implications of it all going horribly wrong.

- ◎ Am I able to get off the wave before it breaks over rocks?

- ◎ Do I have the skill to select the last wave in a set?

- ◎ Am I guaranteed not to swim?

- ◎ Is my third party liability insurance up to date?

After taking everything into account, surfing is still great fun. When surfing waves in overfalls or in a following sea you don't have any swimmers to worry about. Surf beaches are a relatively safe place to learn to handle and roll your kayak in turbulent conditions. Pick a deserted beach well away from other water users… and have fun!

PLATE XXVI *Pirouette! Playtime at Penrhyn Mawr.*
Photo: Johan Wagner www.seakayakingcornwall.com

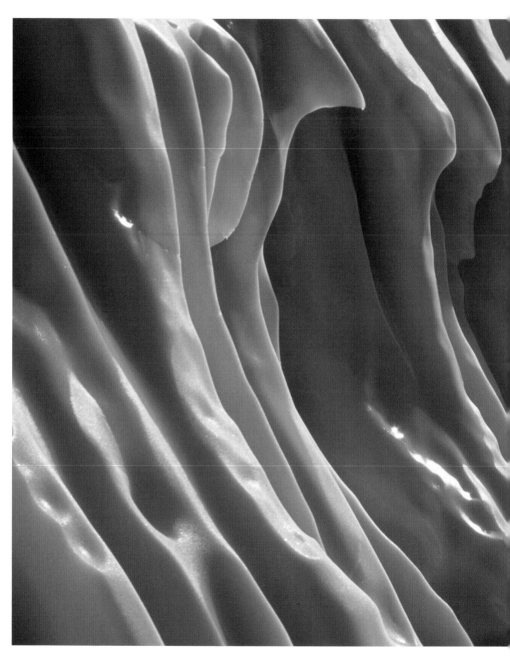

PLATE XXVII *Very regular yet highly abstract patterns can be a feature of natural processes.*

PLATE XXVIII *Exploring North East Skye.*

17 Rockhopping

Rockhopping is a fun activity in itself, although when you participate as a normal part of your sea kayaking, the benefits are huge. From timing to edging under pressure and from reading the water to rescues carried out in double quick time, all these skills and more are developed and honed. This is a great way to improve the whole repertoire of skills required in a sea kayak.

**Reading the water is a skill
which comes only with experience
– but makes everything easier.**

There are many issues when considering an activity such as this. Firstly the kayak you use should be sturdy enough to stand up to the stresses that will be put on it. Obviously, if you land hard on a rock then there is the likelihood of some damage, not only to the boat but also yourself. If you are in the unlikely position of being out of control and surfing towards a rock wall you have a couple of options: capsize and wait until the wave passes, roll up then get away from the mess, or… bail out on the seaward side of your kayak and watch as it breaks into a styrene flavoured jigsaw.

Choice is important, wearing a helmet is a personal thing, some do and some don't. What is important is to be happy with your choice and stick with it. Personal protection is an area that deserves a book to itself. There are no rights or wrongs, only choices. To start though, a helmet is probably a good idea.

Your paddle too should be able to stand up to the stresses of use. There is a greater chance of jamming it between rocks when you are in this zone than for most of the other paddling you will be doing. I always use the same paddle no matter how close inshore I intend going, even if I do end up trying to reshape the blade. On these grounds it seems like a good idea to have some spare paddles throughout the group. If you have a breakdown paddle it may be possible to carry a complete set of spare parts.

The clothing required is no different to what you would normally use when kayaking on the sea; if you like to wear a wetsuit use that, if you are more a drysuit type of person that is fine too. One addition that might be useful is a pair of neoprene diver's gloves. These give some protection from barnacles, mussels and sharp edges should you have to palm off a rock to keep your balance, but they reduce the feel you have on the paddle shaft.

17.1 WHAT IS SAFE?

This is probably the most subjective question you could ask. Bear in mind that what excites one person scares another and has the third contemplating knitting as a hobby!

What you have to remember is that there comes a time when you could well have a swim very close to rocks with water breaking over them. One idea might be to consider swimming in the impact zone before venturing into a serious rockhopping session. At least you will know what it feels like when you get close to the rock.

SIMPLE DO'S & DONT'S:

- As a swimmer, make sure your feet are toward the rock and you are in a position to be able to push away if you have to.

- Never ever let yourself get between your empty kayak and the rock. When the cockpit area is full of water an otherwise empty kayak will weigh around 250kg.

17.2 GETTING CLOSER

You may recall from Chapter 12 that water which is dark coloured is only moving up and down. Water which is aerated and light coloured is flowing somewhere (up, down, left, right, etc.). Choose your spot so that there is dark water moving up and down the rock face. Sit close to the rock and feel how the kayak moves but seldom gets close to touching, there will be a place where things just seem to get calm and you will be capable of sitting in one place without moving too much apart from up and down.

A COUPLE OF GENERAL OBSERVATIONS:

- Edging away from a nearby threatening rock will tend to steer you towards where you do not want to be.

- Edging towards the rock will send you away from the impact zone, although your head and body appear much closer to the danger.

When edging toward the rocks, if you should end up against the rock you are at least in a position to slide and not roll down the face. Make sure you keep edging towards the rock though!

Sometimes you will find yourself very close to the rock and unable to put in a forward stroke on that side, some form of modified stroke will be required. A J-stroke (borrowed from canoeists) is probably the easiest to perform quickly:

J-stroke – a modified forward stroke on one side, with a turning component to allow paddling on one side only. Begin with your standard forward catch, try to use the paddle as vertically as possible, this will reduce any tendency to turn away from the side you are paddling on. Shortly before you exit the stroke, rotate the paddle so that the drive face is facing away from your kayak and lever it slightly away from the boat until the boat responds with a slight turn toward your on-side.

fig. 17.1
Timing is everything – getting it wrong can leave you in a compromising position.

Watch out to sea continuously, observe what is happening and assess what is about to come your way. Always watch an area for more than one or two waves before venturing into the jaws of the monster. This is because waves come in sets, a few small ones are followed by a few big ones. It could be that the larger waves are behaving very differently from the smaller waves.

Work hard at holding your position when you are close to the rocks, this will enable you to stay aligned with your chosen gap while waiting for the right wave. When you have committed to your manoeuvre, be bold and labour to make it happen. Attempt to move in straight lines wherever possible.

Look at the water not the rock. It almost seems stupid to say this. If you think you are going to hit the rock you will. This is much the same as you see yourself missing the nail with your hammer and mashing your thumb instead. I've managed both the rock and the thumb thing on several occasions.

When turning choose either a safe area, or use your momentum. A low brace/reverse sweep combination turn carried out with your kayak well over is probably the best to choose here as you get a lot of stability from the blade in the water. The water behind a reef may be useful as a safe area if it is deep enough and not too close to the next rock or reef. Although relatively chaotic the power of the swell has been broken up. One thing you will have to remember is that the aerated water can be much less supportive than you are used to.

Keep in mind that the swell will come through in sets, with there being periods of bigger waves, this will result in louder sucking and bigger crashing noises. Another consequence is that there is a lot more power in the water to be dissipated by your body and boat.

Paddling through gaps is usually less risky than catching a wave over the top of a rock. When surfing through gaps or over reefs it is best to be going from deep dark water and ending up in deep dark water.

SURF OVER THE TOP OF A REEF:

Start close – allowing you to observe what is happening and choose your time to commit. If you are too far away then you will make a bad judgement call and one of two things will happen: your kayak will turn broadside and you will most likely get some barnacle rash on your head as you capsize onto the rock. You will then be dragged in this inverted position until the wave has played enough with you. Alternatively your kayak will drop off the back of the wave and you will have completed an almost perfect seal landing, only the next wave is already on its way with your name written all over its snarling face.

Go against it – Always try to paddle out through gaps and arches against the direction of the swell, at least the first couple of times, rather than going with it. This allows you to see what is happening and get an idea of the layout of the area, rather than be surfed out of control into some rock or wall which will undoubtedly be far more impervious than either you or your kayak.

PLATE XXIX *Getting close!*

PLATE XXX *A typical overfall off Skye.*

18 Tides & Tidal Races

Tidal race paddling is very similar to river paddling, although when the kayak you are sitting in is something like five metres long instead of under two, things are not quite the same. Anything that involves turning takes a bit longer and your stomach muscles are going to be working an awful lot harder.

To be able to paddle in a tidal race you have to be able to predict when things are going to happen. What information do you need and where do you find this information? Well, you have to know some basics about flow rates and speeds, a bit about timings of start of flow as well as what shipping uses the area. The best place to find out this type of information is within any guidebook that is aimed specifically at sea kayaking; failing that publications aimed at other small-craft water users is alright.

18.1 PLANNING FOR TIDES

Almanac – Of varying use depending on type. Some have tidal gates for well-used areas while others have local information not contained in other publications. All have tide tables for various standard ports as well as local tidal differences.

Pilot – Different publications give different information but generally all give time of tide starting to flow, maximum rate of flow as well as direction, some give a tidal constant which enables you to work out the time of high (or low) water. Most of the tidal stream information is situated offshore, which is where the larger boats that use these books operate. With limited information close to headlands and around shallow areas, all have information that is more suited to larger vessels although much of the pilotage is also useful to us.

Chart – Nautical charts have tidal information published on critical areas. This information takes the form of a table, which relates to a geographical position marked on the chart by a 'tidal diamond'. The information contained within this table is more correct than that given within the tidal stream atlas. Quoting hours before and hours after high water, the rate in knots, and direction in degrees is stated. Also given is the average neap and spring rate.

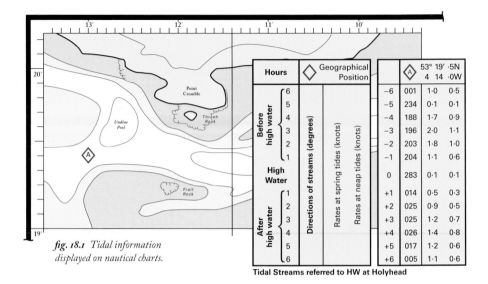

fig. 18.1 Tidal information
displayed on nautical charts.

Hours		Geographical Position					53° 19′ ·5N
							4 14 ·0W
		Directions of streams (degrees)	Rates at spring tides (knots)	Rates at neap tides (knots)			
Before high water	6				−6	001	1·0 0·5
	5				−5	234	0·1 0·1
	4				−4	188	1·7 0·9
	3				−3	196	2·0 1·1
	2				−2	203	1·8 1·0
	1				−1	204	1·1 0·6
High Water					0	283	0·1 0·1
After high water	1				+1	014	0·5 0·3
	2				+2	025	0·9 0·5
	3				+3	025	1·2 0·7
	4				+4	026	1·4 0·8
	5				+5	017	1·2 0·6
	6				+6	005	1·1 0·6

Tidal Streams referred to HW at Holyhead

SPRINGS & NEAPS

As the position of the earth, moon and sun change so does their gravitational effect on the waters of the earth. Although the sun's effect is less than half that of the moon, when these two bodies are in alignment and pulling in the same plane they cause higher high tides and lower low tides, which are called **spring** tides.

The converse of this are **neap** tides. When the sun and moon form a right angle about the earth, there is a cancelling effect and you get lower high tides and higher low tides.

A good rule of thumb is that the **neap** range is half that of the **spring** and as a result the **neap** rate is half the spring flow. This can be seen in the tidal diamond shown above.

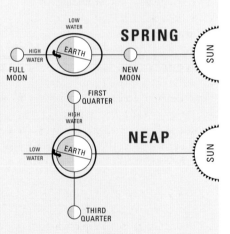

fig. 18.2 (above) The combined tidal effects of the sun and moon.

You may observe a delay between the phases of the moon and its tidal effect, as the earth's tides must travel outward from the southern oceans. In the North Sea, there is a two day lag between the new/full moon and the spring tide. High tides occur every 12 hours 24 minutes – as the earth rotates relative to the moon every 24 hours 48 minutes (a lunar day). Springs and neaps occur approximately every 7.4 days – as the time between two full moons is roughly 29.5 days.

Tidal stream atlas – These give an hour-by-hour pictorial overview of what is happening to the flow of water around a given area of coastline. The times are relative to a standard port although this differs for each atlas. Two numbers separated by a comma are the neaps and springs rate, the arrow gives the direction and approximate speed, a longer heavier arrow indicates a faster current than a shorter lighter one. Speeds quoted are in tenths of a knot, therefore 21,43 suggests a neap rate of 2.1 knots and a spring rate of 4.3 knots. The location of the comma is also the approximate geographical position of the observation. These give reasonable inshore information but perhaps not the detail that we require in a sea kayak.

Paddling guides – While some guides are very good and give good representation of tidal flows and eddies, the direction of flow along with start and finish times, others have less information. As always it is a good idea to use any guidebook with caution. Use your own knowledge, work out the tides for yourself and apply your own set of criteria to your findings in order to determine the suitability of your chosen location.

fig. 18.3 All sorts of publications provide tidal information resources.

Web-based resources – Many of the resources above can now be found on the web.

Locals (and/or paddlers) – A ferryman or fisherman who has worked across the tide will have a better idea of what is actually happening than any written information. He has an idea of what the weather conditions do to the tide to affect its speed and duration. He will also know of any areas that are best to be avoided, although this will probably indicate where the best overfalls are for us to play in.

It is best not to be intimidated by reports of very fast and dangerous tidal streams. Although the people who give this information mean well they probably have little or no experience of how a sea kayak performs. They are also very likely to be coming from another area of boating that is not as able as a kayak to seek out the shallow, inshore routes that only we can.

fig. 18.4 Local knowledge can be invaluable as well as interesting.

I remember when paddling in New Zealand and heading towards a tidal race called French Pass, off the south end of D'Urville Island, a local warned us not to go near the flow as people with thousands of hours kayaking experience had struggled and come to grief. We were on holiday, paddling a huge double, and had no intention of doing anything other than having a bit of fun. Sure the flow was moving in our direction but because we had an idea about tides, we paddled through on the last of the flood, landed and ate lunch then returned on the first of the ebb.

18.2   RULE OF THIRDS & 50-90

There are a couple of rules of thumb when we look to the speed of the current throughout its flow cycle:

Rule of thirds – States that over the period of the first hour the current will flow at one third of its maximum rate (for that day), for the second hour it will flow at two-thirds and the third hour at approximately three-thirds (full speed). This then reduces in similar fashion, during the fourth hour at three-thirds, the fifth hour at two-thirds, and the sixth hour at one third of maximum flow (1 2 3 3 2 1). So as an example, if the maximum rate was a convenient three knots, a log dropped in the water would drift two nautical miles over the period of the second hour.

50-90 rule – This helps to calculate the speed of the current at the end of each hour. The start of the first hour is slack water. At the end of the first hour the current flows at 50% of its maximum rate (for that day), the second hour at 90% and the third hour at 100%. At the end of the fourth hour it will reduce to 90% of the maximum rate, at the end of the fifth hour to 50% and at the end of the sixth hour it will be slack.

Sometimes the flood lasts longer than the ebb and sometimes it is the other way about. Be aware that the thirds rule may not be a good guide to any place where the coastline is very complex and there are bays with multiple or narrow entrances. As an example, instead of the usual 1 2 3 3 2 1 over a roughly six hour period, you may find that in one direction the tide flows over a seven hour period and flows at its strongest for the first two hours! In these locations you will need to study your sources of information carefully and use your own powers of observation.

Certainly on the west coast of Scotland, due to the glaciations that have taken place, most sea lochs or fiords have a shallow area where the fiord meets the open water. This sill can have quite an effect on the tidal flow and in some cases can cause tidal rapids to form such as those at Falls of Lora, just north of Oban.

If you plan to expedition somewhere well off the beaten track it is unlikely that you will be able to find any information about the tidal flow rates. However, by using your knowledge gained from your local waters you should be able to make an educated guess as to what is most likely happening at any given place and time. Where the current does not flow in a regular manner this information is normally found in one of the above publications.

18.3 SPEED OF THE TIDAL STREAM

There are many times when you need to know what speed the tide is flowing at on any given day at a particular time. When planning a journey that involves a route through a narrow gap where there is known to be strong tidal streams, it makes sense to time your passage to coincide with the flow going in your direction. Sometimes you would not want to be in a situation where the flow was building (eg. going through the Gulf of Corryvreckan from east to west with a westerly swell running). At these times it can be beneficial to arrive at the critical area as the flow in your favour is slackening off and then changing direction to flow against you. This would mean that although having to paddle against the start of the flow against you, there is less chance of encountering the extreme water conditions there may be during the main part of the flow.

A FEW METHODS OF ESTIMATING THE RATE OF THE CURRENT

Computation of rates – There is a graph inside the front cover of any Admiralty tidal streams atlas. To use this, find where you want to find the speed of the tidal stream, mark the neap speed and spring speed then join these marks and carry the line beyond both marks. Next work out the range at Dover for the chosen day, look along the line for that range and where the diagonal and horizontal lines intersect is the approximate speed of the tide.

Percentage method – The information in the pilot gives the speed of the tidal stream at mean springs. We can find what the mean range is for our given standard port from an almanac. If tidal range is 70% of mean spring range assume the current to be 70% of mean spring flow. By calculating the range on a chosen day we can work out the percentage difference and then apply this to our rate. The formula would look like:

$$approximate\ tidal\ rate\ (kn) = \frac{given\ tidal\ range\ (m)}{mean\ spring\ range\ (m)} \times mean\ spring\ rate\ (kn)$$

With most sea kayakers being practical people, the methods above work well when at the planning stage and before getting on the water. When on the water things change and you do not have access to all of our tabletop exercise information so you have to use different methods for working out the speed of the tide.

Relative physical effort – If you know what it feels like to paddle at three knots and you are putting in the same amount of relative physical effort without moving forwards against the current, assume that the tide is going three knots.

Passing a fixed point – If you have a five metre kayak and it takes two seconds to pass a fixed point you are travelling at approximately two knots. If you know what it feels like to paddle at three knots and you are putting in the same amount of relative physical effort you must be paddling against a one knot current.

18.4 MANOUEVRING IN A TIDAL RACE

FERRY ANGLE IN RELATION TO THE CURRENT

If you have a good idea of your paddling speed then a general rule to estimate angle of attack would be: If the current is flowing perpendicular to your direction of travel allow 20° for every knot of flow if your paddling speed is three knots, 15° if four knots and 12° if five knots. This gives a reasonable angle up to one knot below your paddling speed as can be seen in the table opposite.

fig. 18.5 Calculating ferry angle.

	Paddling speed (kn)		
	3	4	5
Current (kn) 1	20°	15°	12°
2	40°	30°	24°
3	–	45°	36°
4	–	–	48°

This is very obviously a generalisation and for critical tidal crossings more accurate calculations must be carried out using vectors. This can be done either hourly or as a cumulative plot. For detailed instructions on how to carry this out study *Sea Kayak Navigation* by Franco Ferrero[†]. This concise book gives you what you need, no more, no less.

Vectors are the large-scale, macro calculations that need to be employed in the planning of open crossings with significant tidal flow. As ferrying generally relates to crossing shorter distances, there is a reactive quality to it and this could be seen as a micro vector.

† *Sea Kayak Navigation,* Franco Ferrero, Pesda Press (1999) ISBN 0-9531956-1-9

EDGING & LEANING

Edging, or leaning, when travelling at the same speed as the current, (ie. drifting) has no effect on stability or the chance of catching an edge. Only when at the interface between flow and eddy do they have greatest effect. Described below are methods for dealing with this interface, familiar to river paddlers as breaking in and breaking out.

18.5 BREAK-IN

When going from the eddy into the flow there is a good chance that you will be going to turn and face downstream. There are two methods described below; the first is suited to heavier water when you want to gain maximum support from the paddle. The second is suited to more moderate water where your balance can be used. For both methods make sure the kayak is travelling through the water quickly enough to enable it to make it all the way out of the eddy and into the flow without stalling on the interface.

❶ **Safe option** – Forward sweep as your feet cross the eddy line, turn your head and shoulders and look to where you want the front of the kayak to end up. The best way to continue this turn is to have enough inside edge that allows the waterline length to change but doesn't destabilise the kayak. Engage all of your lower body by pushing on the footrest with the outside foot and press with both thighs on the braces. Use whatever stroke fits your purpose best from low brace, bow rudder, cross-bow rudder or just balance.

figs. 18.6–8 Breaking into the flow, looking and leaning downstream, low brace position.

❷ **Efficient option** – A slightly higher risk alternative is to get the kayak to a position where your feet are about to cross the eddy line. Edging upstream this time, forward sweep on the upstream side still looking at your finish position, have your blade in a low brace position on the upstream side of the kayak. This allows the kayak to turn more efficiently but is less stable, especially when there is a big current differential. Maintain your edge by keeping your weight well over the centre of buoyancy (CB).

18.6 BREAK-OUT

Going from the main current into the eddy. This is most probably the fastest turn you can make in a sea kayak if you have any hull speed and are prepared to lean a long way into the turn. If you get the kayak up to its running speed and aim to hit the eddy about one boat length from the top edge, forward sweep your feet over the interface, get your body weight well forward and immediately drop your inside edge while at the same time applying a hefty dollop of low brace on the inside of the turn. The low brace should be as far away from the centre line of the kayak as is possible to give the greatest effect and slow the boat down. Obviously this turn can also be carried out by using a bow rudder or cross-bow rudder. In this case it is sensible to approach the eddy slightly slower than Mach 4 and to feel the effect of the paddle in the water. Aim to edge towards the outside of the turn immediately the kayak has completely entered the eddy, this enables the boat to turn itself.

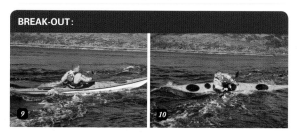

figs. 18.9-10 Breaking out into an eddy with speed and a low brace position, looking and leaning into the eddy.

Photos: Morag Brown

18.7 EDDY LINE SPINS

This is a good exercise in edge awareness. When done well in a sea kayak it is probably the most graceful and energy efficient way of turning using the assistance of the tide.

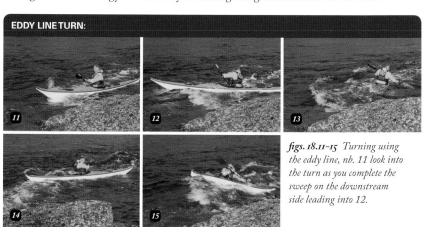

figs. 18.11-15 Turning using the eddy line, nb. 11 look into the turn as you complete the sweep on the downstream side leading into 12.

Using very little forward momentum is good as this allows you to feel what is happening to the boat. Good body rotation, leading with the head, well placed strokes and using the whole body paddling approach.

As the bow of the kayak starts to be turned by the current, wind up into the reverse crunch sweep position, this immediately ensures your weight is in the right position as well as your paddle. Let the current take the boat as far as you want then apply the reverse stroke. This timing ensures you have stability on the reverse sweep whilst leaning 'upstream', change edges as the reverse sweep comes near to the end of its usefulness. By now the bow will be back close to the start point and only requires a forward sweep to take it over the interface (alternatively, slice the working blade forwards and into a bow draw position. By varying the angle of blade to flow you reduce the need for a forward sweep). You should now be in a position to start the sequence again.

It is very easy to ignore your feet and legs when in a high stress situation but as soon as you begin to engage your lower body the boat will almost turn itself.

18.8 EDDYHOPPING UPSTREAM

Using your surroundings to make progress against the tide. Angle of attack is the prime focus for success. If too much angle is used the kayak will peel out of the eddy and into the main current quicker that you would believe, leaving you to sweep on the downstream side for a long time. Too little and there is a fair chance of being washed onto the rocks at the top of the eddy itself. So what is the correct angle to aim for? Something that approaches straight upstream is great, although you will have to be able to read what is actually happening on the eddy/flow interface.

fig. 18.16 Heading out of the eddy pointing well upstream, it may be possible to hug the rocks and make headway upstream.

When paddling in rough water and especially the tidal race environment, you will get more response from your kayak if the skeg is retracted.

A well-known sea kayak coach, when paddling in a Jersey tidal race, was struggling to move upstream into the higher eddy. After having had three or four attempts where his kayak was turned around with the flow, one of the youngsters from the club suggested that if he were to pull the skeg up it would be a bit easier. To say that he was embarrassed would not be exaggerating.

Start the kayak moving upstream and towards the eddy line slightly below where you want to enter the current. Aim to enter almost perpendicular to the flow with your last stroke being a sweep in the current, this will enable your bow to come round and head directly upstream. If this is not too successful then another couple of sweep strokes done very quickly will get you on line.

Hull speed also plays its part. Too slow and the kayak will sit on the eddy line not wanting to make the step into the flow, too fast and it will penetrate well into the flow and risk turning before a corrective stroke can be used.

18.9 MOVING UPSTREAM USING STANDING WAVES

It is possible to surf the upstream faces of standing waves in order to move upstream against a flow that is stronger than you can normally paddle against. Similar to surfing a swell but the chances are that the waves will be steeper and breaking more irregularly.

Wind, waves and tide, when travelling in the same direction, will flatten out a rough sea. When opposed, the waves become closer together, more irregular and break more frequently in unpredictable ways. Swell waves, however, carry through the flow of the tide unabated. A swell will affect the volume of water passing through a standing wavetrain and hence the size and shape of the waves will pulse with the swell.

For a discussion of successfully surfing a wave, see Chapter 16, Surf & Surfing, particularly 16.4, Staying on a wave, where the 'torque' turn is described.

PLATE XXXI *Swell passing through a tidal race will produce exaggerated, surging features.*
Aled Williams at North Stack, Anglesey.
Photos: Franco Ferrero

PLATE XXXII *Ian Wilson using wings in his Inuk during the 'Heb'.*
Photo: Jeff Allen, seakayakingcornwall.com

19 Competition

19.1 GREENLAND KAYAKING CHAMPIONSHIPS

Not all competition relating to sea kayaking involves being the fastest person on the water, indeed some of the more skilful performances are to be seen at the Greenland Kayaking Championships. These 'games' take the form of the training that a Greenlander would have to undergo before becoming a kayaker. As with many other similar nations, these training exercises take the form of feats of strength as well as skill.

Rope gymnastics is a lesser-known part of the preparation for Greenland style rolling. The paddler has to perform a number of manoeuvres on both a single and a double rope suspended above the ground. Scoring is by style and length of time position is maintained.

Within the rolling section there are over thirty different rolls that have to be performed on both sides. Although the modern roll is simply a highly effective way to right yourself after a capsize, the Greenland kayakers of old had to be able to right themselves from any position without letting go of some piece of vital equipment or whilst tangled up in the harpoon line or any other hunting equipment carried on deck.

Harpoon throwing as well as short and long course races make up the remainder of the competition. Competitors are now using drysuits beneath the sealskin 'tuilik' and are having kayaks designed purely to enable specific rolls to be executed. Blade size and shape have also departed from the traditional dimensions in order to make use of the buoyancy and lift properties an increase in size gives.

19.2 ADVENTURE RACING

This fast growing sport sometimes includes sea kayaking as one of the disciplines. There are many such events, a few of the better known ones are; the Eco Challenge, The Wilderness ARC and the Hebridean Challenge. The 'Heb' takes place on the Outer Hebrides and the organisers insist on a minimum standard of participant, this generally relates to time spent on the water and can include awards such as British Canoe Union four star (sea kayak).

With classes of entry from team to individual competitor, these races can be of one day to five in duration. Some of the harder races are continuous in nature with the winning team being that which finishes first having completed all the challenges.

fig. 19.1
Hybrid race /
sea kayaks in
the Hebridean
Challenge.
Photo:
Jeff Allen

Photo: seakayakingcornwall.com

The kayaks that have evolved for these events are sophisticated craft. More like a racing kayak than a sea kayak but with features, such as hatches and bulkheads, that allow them to fit within the rules. The top competitors are averaging over twelve kilometres an hour, which in most sea kayakers' terms, is about twice normal paddling speed.

19.3 CHALLENGES

Although it would be fair to say there are few 'new' challenges, there are a number of existing records for crossings. Many of these are unofficial and down to the paddler, their choice of weather and craft but there are others that are tightly scrutinised.

THE ENGLISH CHANNEL: The Guinness record for crossing the Channel is held by Ian Tordoff who completed the thirty-five kilometre crossing in a time of three hours, twenty-one minutes and fifty-four seconds on May 18th 2005. The previous record holder for this was Drew Samuel, who lived in the same town I was brought up in. His record stood since 1976 and was untouchable because he had used a racing kayak and was, at the time of the crossing, a full time athlete employed by the RAF. Drew's time was only eleven minutes slower than Ian's!

NORTH SEA CROSSING: This has been done many times in both single and double kayaks. Franco Ferrero and Kevin Danforth in 1989 paddled an Aleut Sea Two produced by Howard Jeffs and some years earlier Derek Hutchinson and friends made the crossing in single kayaks of his own design.

IRISH SEA CROSSING: There have been many people who have risen to this challenge – best attempted from Wales to Ireland, to arrive on the wide coast of Dublin instead of navigating to the island of Holyhead.

AROUND BRITAIN: Sean Morley's grand tour of all inhabited islands around our coasts in 2004 will stand the test of time as a fantastic challenge.

SHETLAND TO FAEROE ISLANDS: Dan and Karen Trotter, a husband and wife team, attempted to paddle their self-designed 'Torridon' double kayak from Shetland to the Faeroes in 1995. They were beset by problems such as seismic survey ships crossing and re-crossing their path and called it a day only thirty miles from their destination. Their kayak was taken in tow behind their support yacht and broke loose as they approached the islands. It was found two days later close to the Butt of Lewis. A better way to tackle this crossing would be the other way as Shetland is a much bigger target and the tides are much weaker than those off the Faeroes.

HEBRIDEAN & PENTLAND TRIANGLES: Both of these challenges have now been completed. The Hebridean triangle was the last of these to be concluded, and was achieved earlier this year (2006) by Patrick Winterton.

NORTH LEWIS & PENTLAND FIRTH: This is one of those journeys that gets looked at, then dismissed as just silly. Starting from Orkney, head west visiting Sule Skerry and Stack Skerry, continue west to North Rona then Sula Sgeir and finish on Lewis. The main challenge on this is not just the distances involved but the navigation and risk of no available landings when reaching any of the islands, perhaps 'rock' would be a better description! The shuttle from start to finish would also be worthy of the title 'challenge'.

From Lewis to Sula Sgeir and North Rona back to Lewis has been completed by Murty Campbell from Stornoway in 1992. He is the Cox on the RNLI lifeboat there so knows a bit about the sea. Sule Skerry and Stack Skerry have been paddled to from the north coast of Scotland by Archie Waters in 1982. The complete journey has yet to be paddled.

These are just a few of the challenges I believe there are around the coast of the British Isles. There are very many more elsewhere in the world and it would be foolish not to include the 'Big Crossings'; the Atlantic Ocean by Hannes Lindeman (1955) and more recently Peter Bray (2001) as well as Monterey to Maui (1987) in the Pacific Ocean by Ed Gillet.

PLATE XXXIII *Toasty toes, North West Greenland.*

20 Overnighting & Expeditions

Whether at home or abroad the sea kayak is the perfect mode of transport for expeditioning. As you don't have to carry any weight on your back it makes sense for long journeys. Anywhere in the world is a potential destination for exploration if you have the time to plan and the required resources to enable you to carry your plan through. An expedition can be whatever you want it to be. For some people it is a weekend and for others it is a few weeks or more.

Rather than give a comprehensive guide to expeditioning I have collected some of my thoughts on the organisational aspects.

20.1 NUMBER OF PEOPLE

Expeditioning alone can mean freedom but also the possibility of loneliness. Two is fun but can become difficult if for a long time. Three is good but can cause splits within the party. Four or more is great as smaller sub-groups can operate without anyone stepping on anyone else's toes.

20.2 TYPE OF KAYAK

What types of kayak are available? Is it possible to transport your own? Will you take a rigid take-apart or folder? Are you prepared to hire whatever is available when you get to your chosen location? Some rental companies tell you anything to ensure you sign up with them, always try to make sure you have a written agreement as to exactly what you are and are not getting. If you are renting a car as well as kayaks, does the car have a roofrack or are you taking your own along? In an emergency, is there any public transport that you could use? Are you able to fly in and out of your start point or will you be able to get there by boat?

figs. 20.1-2 Folding kayak (top) vs take-apart (bottom), neither of which are inexpensive options.

20.3 EQUIPMENT

For a month long expedition I would not take very much more than if I were going for a week. A good idea is to take as little as possible but as much as you need. The result of this is that you spend less time packing and unpacking your kit and more time exploring and watching the wildlife. Some things are fairly obvious such as a larger tent just in case the weather forces a period of time spent inside. A tarp is a great addition especially if there is a group of you, it can be used for cooking under as well as sheltering from rain or even sun and it is also excellent for socialising.

KIT MANAGEMENT

When I come ashore at the end of a day's paddle I do not get changed straight away, instead preferring to keep on any damp kit. This ensures that the dampness dries a little and I can keep my dry stuff dry. Obviously, if you are the type of person who does get cold when you stop exercising, then your approach will be different; perhaps an additional wind and waterproof layer will be enough for you. Some folk like to expedition in a drysuit but I find them quite uncomfortable if I have to wear one for any length of time. My one luxury when away on any length of expedition is a dry pair of wool socks, I keep these for when I get into the tent and after drying my feet they go on and stay in place until I am heading outside again. A good idea is to have a couple of polythene bags that you can put over the dry socks if the weather is really poor.

I always carry a complete set of clothing for use when I am in the tent, it doesn't ever get wet, and if I want to go outside I will put my kayaking kit back on and deal with the elements that way.

For everything you take make sure that you have spares of the things that are likely to break and are able to be repaired in the field (that is assuming you are capable of attempting a repair in the first place!), e.g. stove repair kit, thermarest repair kit, tent repair including pole sleeves (perhaps spare poles) batteries for whatever you use that requires them (perhaps a solar charger if your plans are at all grand). Every possibility of damage that is likely to occur will happen whether you are close to home or in a distant corner of the world so it is best practice to always carry the resources that will allow you to effect a satisfactory repair.

20.4 BODY FUEL

What food you take depends on where you are going, how long your expedition will be and whether you can resupply en-route or not. Tinned foods are obviously heavy but they are generally already cooked so could be eaten without heating if you absolutely had to. Dehydrated or freeze dried meals are good for weight saving and some of them have become quite palatable, or perhaps my memory of them has diminished, either way you can pack a lot more into a smaller place if you go down this line. Pasta and rice are good to take along, especially if you can get hold of the quick cook varieties that are available. Condiments are also a must, from soy sauce to flaked chillies, I have found that on trips I like stronger flavours than I would usually have at home. Remember that no matter what type of foodstuffs you opt for, the rubbish will need to be stored and brought home.

20.5 DISTANCE

Probably one of the main considerations will be that of how far to paddle in a day. My recommendation would be an average of ten to fifteen miles as this allows for bad weather and other eventualities. This is not to say that you are limited to these figures, shorter distances allow for exploring the area you are visiting which is probably part of the reason for you being there in the first place. If you are planning on thirty-mile days, you don't have to be a rocket scientist to work out that you will have a lot of catching up to do if you get bad weather for a few days.

fig. 20.3 *Amongst ice today. Where next?*

20.6   COMMUNICATION

Bearing in mind that most sea kayak expeditions take place in a remote setting, some means of summoning outside assistance should be carried in the event of something untoward happening. That said, when I am on expedition, I don't carry much more than my mobile phone and VHF radio, both of which are switched off, although the VHF is handy on deck and not in a hatch!

20.7   REMOTE PLACES

For some expeditions in remote places, you have to get a permit, in addition the authorities demand that you carry a satellite phone with you and also that you call in each evening at a pre-determined time. For expeditions in Tierra Del Fuego and Southern Chile it is mandatory that you obtain a permit one year in advance and that you also have the appropriate level of insurance to allow a rescue to be carried out[†].

In some locations you are obliged to have large vessel back-up. The obvious location that springs to mind is South Georgia, there have been two successful circumnavigations over the 2005/2006 season. One group used their support boat for accommodation while the other made sure their rescue party were far enough away that they were not seen.

Many outfitters in these regions can equip you with the required apparatus for a fee. In addition, if you book with a local tour company, they will arrange the necessary documentation as part of their service.

EMERGENCY LOCATOR BEACONS

For remote places - Other options available to you if there is no compulsory carrying of specific equipment are: Emergency Position Indicator Radio Beacon (EPIRB) and Personal Locator Beacon (PLB). Both these systems require information to be relayed to the appropriate rescue authority. From the time you activate the unit until likely rescue can be anything from 10 hours to 20 days depending on your location on the globe. The one downside to these is that you do not know if anyone has received your distress call.

† *Sea Kayaking*, Jonathan Hanson,
Outside Books (2001) ISBN 0-393-32070-7

20.8 LANGUAGE

For most locations around the world, the English language will get you what you want. Although in China and South America as well as the more remote Pacific and Arctic areas you will struggle without an interpreter, my feelings are that this is just part of the fun.

> When paddling in the Ummannaq fjord area of north-west Greenland with Duncan Winning, we managed to find out about the halibut fisheries, outboard motor problems, schooling and the history of the village of Igdllorrsuit. In addition we found ourselves invited to kafemik in a house at the other end of the village the next morning at ten. We had no Greenlandic and they had no English or Danish, but we did manage to find out a great deal about life there.

20.9 COST

The cost implications will obviously dictate where you ultimately travel to, a week on the west coast of Scotland can cost as little as your food and fuel costs to get there if you live in the UK, while a month in Antarctica may well cost you more than a year's salary. What it comes down to is your desire to explore a new region, having the necessary capital to realise your dream and having a very understanding partner!

20.10 FIRST AID TRAINING

For extended journeying, I would highly recommend some form of specialist wilderness emergency first aid training as typically, first aid relies on the assumption that professional medical help will arrive within the hour, obviously this is out of the question. Some more information on dealing with typical kayak related injuries can to be found within the Safety & Rescue chapter. Think about your local waters – how long would it take someone to get to you? I know that around Skye the minimum time from contacting the rescue services to arrival on scene is not less than one hour even when in close proximity to roads or villages.

20.11 GATHERING INFORMATION

Before setting out gather knowledge from others who have been before (the web is an increasingly useful tool in this respect). Ask questions that give you the information you require such as: How frequently are there landing areas? What about places to camp? Are there any language difficulties? What is the best time to go? What are the bugs like? Are there any larger animals that are higher up the food chain than me?

fig. 20.4 Sometimes local information is well on display.

The oceans are the most hostile and dynamic environment on earth, they are also very fragile. We know less about the sea than we do about the moon and yet we exploit everything that comes from it. There are creatures living in the deep oceans that have yet to be seen and things happen on the deep sea floor that we don't yet understand.

By journeying and playing on the surface of the ocean we are placing ourselves at its mercy and have to do so on its terms. It would be nice to think that we have some measure of control but that is not so. We have to be aware of its moods, calm or stormy, know how to deal with the challenges it presents and be prepared for any eventuality.

When you live on the sea for many days at a time you become aware of its cycles and can adapt accordingly. Tides come and go, weather systems pass with new ones taking their place, the moon waxes and wanes and the seasons run their course.

Experience counts for everything and there is no alternative but to go out and enjoy the adventures you are given.

If what you have read has gone some way towards helping you understand the sea and you in your kayak upon it, then this book has done its work. I hope that you have enjoyed the journey as much as I have so far, thank you for taking the time to travel with me.

PLATE XXXIV *Don't forget to have fun!*

FURTHER READING

GENERAL:

Canoe and Kayak Handbook, British Canoe Union, Pesda Press (2002) 0-9531956-5-1

Survival at Sea, MacLean T, Century Hutchinson Ltd (1989) 0-09-174017-7

Stretching, Anderson B, Pelham Books (1981) 0-7207-1351-X

NAVIGATION:

Sea Kayak Navigation, Ferrero F, Pesda Press (1999) 0-9531956-1-9

Fundamentals of Kayak Navigation, Burch D, Globe Pequot (1987) 0-87106-516-9

SEA KAYAK SPECIFIC:

A Practical Guide to Sea Canoeing, Jeffs H, Capel Curig (1986) OOP

Sea Kayaking, Dowd J, Douglas & McIntyre Ltd (1988) 0-88894-598-1

Sea Kayaking, Hanson J, Outside Books (2001) 0-393-32070-7

DESIGN:

The Bark Canoes And Skin Boats Of North America, Adney E & Chappelle H, Smithsonian institute press (1983) 1-56098-269-9

Baidarka, Dyson G, Alaska northwest books (1986) 0-88240-315-X

Qajaq, Zimmerly D, State Museum Alaska (1986)

Skinboats of Greenland, Petersen H, Museum of Greenland (1986) 87-85180-084

Stripbuilt Kayaks, Schade N, Ragged Mountain Press (1998) 0-07-057989-X

Building the Greenland Kayak, Cunningham C, Ragged Mountain Press (2003) 0-07-139237-8

Eastern Arctic Kayaks, Heath J & Arima E, University of Alaska Press (2004) 1-889963-25-9

HISTORICAL:

First Crossing Of Greenland, Nansen F, Longmans, Green and Co. (1902)

Seal Folk and Ocean Paddlers, MacAulay J, White Horse Press (1998) 1-974267-39-1

TRAVEL NARRATIVES:

Dances with Waves, Wilson B, The O'Brien Press (1998) 0-86278-551-0

Blazing Paddles, Wilson B, The Oxford Illustrated Press (1998) 0-946609-59-4

Argonauts of the Western Isles, Lloyd-Jones R, Diadem Books Ltd (1989) 0-906371-03-1

HISTORICAL TRAVEL:

The Last of the Cockleshell Heroes, Sparks W & Munn M, Leo Cooper (1992) 0-85052-297-8

Watkins Last Expedition, Chapman S, William Heinemann Ltd (1953)

Kayak to Cape Wrath, Henderson J, William McLennan & Co Ltd (1951)

Quest by Canoe (Glasgow to Skye), Dunnett A, The Travel Book Club

A Thousand Miles in The Rob Roy, MacGregor J (1881)

Alone at Sea, Lindemann H, Menasha Ridge Press (1999) 3925660275

WEATHER:

The Weather Handbook, Watts A, Sheridan House Inc. (2001) 1-57409-081-X

Weather for Hillwalkers and Climbers, Thomas M, Sutton Publishing Ltd. (2002) 0-7509-1080-1

The Skywatchers Handbook, Ronan C & Dunlop S, Bookmart Ltd. (1993) 1-85648-119-0

WEBSITES:

www.magicseaweed.com (swell forecasting)

www.xcweather.co.uk (swell forecasting)

www.fnmoc.navy.mil (swell forecasting)

www.xcweather.co.uk (weather forecasting)

www.meto.gov.uk/inshore (weather forecasting)

www.bbc.com/weather (weather forecasting)

www.seapaddler.co.uk (sea kayaking)

www.ukseakayakguidebook.co.uk (sea kayaking)

VIDEOS:

This is the Sea I & II, Justine Curgenven, Cackle TV (inspirational footage from around the world)

Over... and Out, Gordon Brown, Stable Recordings (sea kayak rescues – now dated)

INDEX